# Praise for *The Best Damn Website & eCommerce Marketing Optimization Guide, Period!*

*This thorough, comprehensive guide is an absolute must-have for any marketer's library. There's countless lessons and tips available for every website, regardless of that digital property's purpose, and it's delivered in a clear, easy-to-digest fashion. Digital marketers of all skill levels - from grizzled website veterans to fresh-faced newbies - will find something of value here.*

**Mordy Oberstein**
Liaison to SEO Comunity, Wix

*Stoney hits another home run. This should be mandatory reading for anyone working within the digital space. This is a blueprint for website success and will change the way you look at website optimization.*

**Alan Waggoner**
Paid Search Marketing Veteran

*Where most search optimizers claim success once a visitor has hit the page, deGeyter keeps going. He starts with the end in mind and then takes the reader into the world of page optimization, where visitors become customers, and fortunes are truly made.*

**Brian Massey**
Conversion Scientist®, Conversion Sciences

*Stoney deGeyter has mastered the art of innovative marketing as both an international leading speaker and author. Stoney shares his personal marketing successes. This book is clear, concise, and able to inspire by opening new ideas.*

**Brett Tabke**
Founder, Pubcon

*I highly recommend you buy this book if you want to get your website working harder for you! Stoney is a respected web professional who explains everything you need to know about improving your website, in understandable language.*

**Anita Campbell**
Founder, Small Business Trends Media

*Stoney has been in the digital marketing space for as long as I can remember. He has a strong passion in sharing his knowledge and expertise with others. I am excited for you to read his next book and learn from one of the masters in this space.*

**Barry Schwartz**
Search Engine Roundtable

*It made me happy to see Stoney suggest optimizing pages for your audience and not the search engines. I also appreciate the emphasis on critical thinking. There are a lot of actionable. relevant, and helpful suggestions in* The Best Damn Website & eCommerce Marketing Optimization Guide, Period!. *If you are learning SEO, you should check this book out.*

**Bill Slawski**
Director of SEO Research, Go Fish Digital

*Don't even start planning or implementing your website before reading this book! In clear, easy-to-understand language, Stoney details the steps you need to take to ensure the search engines love your site – and so do your visitors!*

**David Szetela**
Owner and CEO, FMB Media
President, Paid Search Association

*An accessible guide for beginners and a valuable reference for experienced site owners,* The Best Damn Website & eCommerce Marketing Optimization Guide, Period! *is a solid resource for anyone looking to launch or improve their website.*

**George Nguyen**
Editor, Search Engine Land

*Stoney's new book does not disappoint! It provides a how-to for basic SEO with plenty of tips and good advice that will set any web marketer up for success.*

**Jenny Halasz**
President, JLH Marketing

*Amazingly simple tips that almost every business forgets to do. This book is worth every penny and then some.*

**Joe Pulizzi**
4x Amazon Best-Selling Author including
*Content Inc.* and *Epic Content Marketing*

*Digital marketers of all experience levels will benefit from reading* The Best Damn Website & eCommerce Marketing Optimization Guide, Period!. *Filled with fun, helpful examples and no shortage of details on the "how," this is truly a soup to nuts look at creating a well-organized and optimized website designed to rank in organic search.*

**Katie Tweedy**
Content Marketing and Strategy Supervisor, Nina Hale

*In-depth is an understatement. This isn't some topical "drive-by" attempt to explain website optimization. Stoney addresses the reality that there aren't "cookie-cutter" solutions for everyone and lays EVERYTHING out in equipping you to weigh your options in order to determine what makes the most sense for your unique website.*

**Seth Tachick**
Marketing Director, Blank Shirts, Inc.

*Successfully optimizing a website is 80% basics and 20% "the rest". If you can get that 80% right, you're most likely going to be ahead of your competition. This book gives you the knowledge to get to that 80% level, and then takes a foray into the 20%.*

**Simon Heseltine**
VP of Audience Growth, Trader Interactive

*Want to know the "how" of driving massive traffic to your site? Stoney is an experienced veteran who breaks down the nuts and bolts of SEO and good web usability. Get this book before your competitors do!*

**Tim Ash**
Keynote Speaker, Marketing Advisor
Bestselling Author of *Unleash Your Primal Brain*

*With* The Best Damn Website & eCommerce Marketing Optimization Guide, Period! *Stoney deGeyter once again proves there's no substitute for experience. Though many of Stoney's recommendations are tried and true, he also gives the reader ideas for how to deal with some of the newer, tricky situations in modern website designs. From keyword selection all the way to conversion optimization, this is a very useful guide for marketers looking to get the greatest leverage from their greatest online asset: their website.*

**Will Scott**
CEO, Search Influence

*I'm a fan of Stoney deGeyter's books. He is knowledgeable and methodical. What he presents in* The Best Damn Website & eCommerce Marketing Optimization Guide, Period! *is evergreen. Stoney is up to date but won't bore you with arcane details. He provides a thorough how-to guide that will serve you well today and in the future. Don't just buy this book, study it, and implement what it recommends.*

**Jeffrey Eisenberg**
CEO, Buyer Legends CEO
2x NY Times Bestselling Author

# The Best Damn Website & eCommerce Marketing Optimization Guide, Period!

by Stoney deGeyter

The Best Damn Website & eCommerce Marketing Optimization Guide, Period!

© 2021 by Stoney deGeyter

Published by: Stoney deGeyter

Books may be purchased by contacting the publisher and author at:
stoneywritesstuff@gmail.com

Cover Design by: Macey Cave

Editors: Jenny Halasz

Proofreaders: Mackenzie Leigh Lusby, Juanell Hopper, Frances Andrew, LeeAnn Imel-Hartford, Tim Radle

deGeyter, Stoney, 1972-

The Best Damn Website & eCommerce Marketing Optimization Guide, Period!

Library of Congress Control Number: xxxxx

1. Business 2. Internet 3. Digital Marketing

ISBN 9798709843851

First Edition Printed in the United States of America

# TABLE OF CONTENTS

Foreword ........................................................................................................ 1

Introduction: ................................................................................................. 2

Keyword Research .......................................................................................... 4

Domain Name & URL Structure ................................................................... 22

Link & Navigation Optimization .................................................................. 32

Title Tag Optimization .................................................................................. 54

Meta Tag Optimization .................................................................................. 60

Heading Tag Optimization ............................................................................ 66

Duplicate Content Issues .............................................................................. 70

Conversion Optimization .............................................................................. 84

Product Category Page Optimization ........................................................... 90

Product Page Optimization ......................................................................... 102

Structured Data Optimization ..................................................................... 116

PDF Optimization ........................................................................................ 122

Concluding Remarks .................................................................................... 132

About the Author ......................................................................................... 134

# FOREWORD

Stoney deGeyter's new book, *The Best Damn Website & eCommerce Marketing Optimization Guide, Period!*, sets high expectations - and does not disappoint.

The website is recognized as one of the most valuable assets of any brand. Optimization is essential to realizing return on investments made in the website as well marketing investments, on - and offline.

Website and eCommerce optimization are complex, everchanging topics that challenge business leaders, website, marketing, IT and design professionals of all levels. Many books have been written on SEO, the default term for website optimization. Yet, few books decipher the technical aspects of optimization and dive into the optimization process the way Stoney does in this book.

*The Best Damn Website & eCommerce Marketing Optimization Guide, Period!* explains how audiences use the internet, then offers specific, actionable steps that optimize the website far beyond the concept of keywords to elevate the website's ability to serve audiences and deliver *results*.

Stoney uses real-world examples to illustrate *what* optimization is, *why* it is essential, and *how* to optimize one's website to compete in today's saturated digital marketplace.

*The Best Damn Website & eCommerce Marketing Optimization Guide, Period!* is Stoney's sequel to *The Best Damn Web Marketing Checklist, Period!*; a book I highly recommend with confidence to entrepreneurs and marketers. Together, these books enable readers to apply decades of real-world experience to help readers leverage the website and internet marketing to grow their brand with confidence.

It takes many years to aggregate the first-hand experience and in-depth knowledge on the many aspects of optimization that Stoney has condensed into these valuable resources.

The digital landscape waits for no one. There are literally only two choices:

1. Take the time to learn by trial and error; or
2. Save countless hours and implement guidance from an experienced, respected marketing expert.

These books just might be the best investments you make in your business this year.

Rebecca Murtagh – author of *Million Dollar Websites: Build a Better Website Using Best Practices of the Web Elite in E-Business, Design, SEO, Usability, Social, Mobile and Conversion*

# INTRODUCTION:

## Your Website Matters

When it comes to building your online presence there is only one logical place to start: your website. Your website is you. You own it. You control it.

Any presence you build outside of your website isn't yours to keep. It may be a reflection of you, but when the lights go out on any entity you don't fully own or control, a piece of you disappears with it.

What happens if Facebook cancels your account? Or Twitter bans you from their platform? Can you get your content back?

Nope. It's gone forever. And most of the time, without an opportunity to appeal. All your hard work building your web presence is wiped out with a snap of the fingers.

This is why you need to have a website to call "home." If your web host turns off the lights, no problem. Take your backups to a new web host and turn them back on again.

You control your website. You—and only you—decide your fate. Which means you get to decide how deep, how wide, and how tall to build your web presence.

You can't do that with any other online platform. Your website is the most critical part of building a successful and effective web presence.

## Build a Winning Web Presence

Anyone who has been involved in digital marketing for any length of time can attest that one of the most critical factors of online success is Search Engine Optimization (SEO). I don't care much for the term SEO because we don't optimize search engines. That's what the algorithm tweakers at Google do.

We optimize websites. It just so happens that we optimize them for search engines, but we optimize them for our visitors as well. I would also argue that optimizing for visitors is far more important than optimizing for Google or Bing. That's not to say search engines aren't important. They are. However, search engines are not your customers. They don't buy your products or services, or click on your ads, people do. And that makes optimizing your website for people the most important thing you can do.

The good news is, it's not an either/or situation. You optimize for both search engines and visitors at the same time. Great search engine optimization is just great visitor optimization. If you think about it, Google's only job is to provide highly relevant links to searchers based on what they are looking for. Or, to put it more succinctly, deliver access to websites that their searchers will love.

Historically, digital marketers have considered top rankings to be the goal of their optimization efforts. That's flawed logic. Rankings are not the goal, they are the reward for a job well done. A top search engine ranking is the trophy for having a website that your audience loves. Google doesn't make the winners; it simply rewards them.

Want to create a website that resonates? One that searchers and visitors find worthwhile? Then this book is for you.

There's not enough paper in the world to cover every aspect of website optimization. Nonetheless, the book you are reading is a comprehensive guide to mastering the art of website optimization. I have no doubt that you will find it valuable as you push forward in your optimization efforts.

# KEYWORD RESEARCH

Keyword research is one of the most crucial elements of a successful digital marketing campaign. While there are many important components to consider to successfully market your website (such as links, website architecture, content, etc.), keyword research tops the list of foundational essentials. Not because the research itself moves the needle, but because every aspect of your digital marketing campaign comes back to your audience and how they think of your product or service.

Throughout this chapter, we'll use a fictional website called *Bags! Bags! Bags!* to demonstrate the keyword research process. We will use real examples of research performed at the time of this writing.

There is no one "right" way to perform keyword research, but there are many key things that you must do to ensure that your research is useful for executing an effective campaign.

## Phase I: Uncovering Core Terms

Many people think of keyword research as the process of looking for keywords to optimize. That is certainly part of the total process, but you'll never be able to systematically discover every relevant keyword until you have a firm grasp of your core terms.

Years ago, the conventional wisdom was that you couldn't successfully optimize a page for more than three keywords. This three-keyword theory came from a fundamental misunderstanding of what good content is, and how to be effective at optimizing it. Thankfully, that flawed thinking is long gone.

It wasn't until Google's Hummingbird update in 2013 that the SEO community realized that one can optimize webpage content for more than a few keywords/phrases at a time. However, this type of optimization is only effective when you think about optimizing your pages by topic rather than by keyword.

Start your keyword research process by uncovering these topics that are represented by core terms. This allows you to set the foundation for an effective, long-term optimization strategy that helps you write exactly the kind of content searchers are looking for.

## Core Terms Defined: What to Look For

Let's start by defining what a core term is (and isn't) so you know what to look for as you start your research. Think of a core term as a word or short phrase that represents a particular topic. Let's take our fictional travel bag ecommerce website *Bags! Bags! Bags!* as an example. Researching the word *bags* will return thousands of results ranging from sandwich bags to sleeping bags, many of which may not all be relevant to our sample site. But within those results, you're likely to find dozens of relevant core terms you can use for deeper research.

The core term acts as the primary representation of a particular topic. In the illustration below, you can see that the single word bag is too broad to be useful as a core term, so we use it as a seed to find core terms that our fictional site *Bags! Bags! Bags!* can work with.

*Illustration by Stoney deGeyter*

Typically, a core term will be a two-word phrase without any qualifiers, though, depending on the topic, they can be comprised of one or even three or more words. While you don't want your core terms to be too broad, you also don't want them to be too specific. For instance, *travel duffel bags with wheels* isn't a good core term. It's far too specific and doesn't help you find more relevant phrases, which is the goal of the core term research phase.

The best core terms contain only one more word beyond what would make the phrase too broad (*duffel bag* vs *bag*.) Core terms maintain a balance between being so broad that they are useless and too specific that they qualify as a search phrase (we'll get to those later). Core terms help us find search phrases in the next phase, so here we try to avoid those.

Unfortunately, defining a core term precisely is difficult as guidelines for what makes a good core term in one industry may not apply to the next. This leaves a bit of ambiguity that you will learn to manage as we go through the full keyword research process.

## Step 1: Research and Discovery

Keyword research tools are an important part of the core term discovery process, however, we're not ready to dive into them just yet. We need to start with some basic research.

Begin by using core terms you know and then dig around to find the first batch of search phrases. After you find these, you can use your research tools to find the search phrases you don't know. Here are a few good places to start:

**Content of your own** – Regardless of how well you think you know your website content, it's a good idea to review it. Who knows what will jump out at you? Scan each page and make a list of any core term candidates you find. Pay special attention to tags, page content, navigation, and unique product names.

**Creative thinking** – a.k.a. brainstorming. It may seem strange that this comes second, but there's no use racking your brain for something you can easily find in your own website's content. This step works best by sitting down with a few other people and brainstorming ideas that you haven't already written down. You can grease the wheels of this brainstorming session by asking and answering questions that your website may not answer:

- What is your average customer looking for?
- What are your visitors trying to accomplish?
- What can you find in Thesauri, taxonomies, and ontologies?
- What words are used in industry glossaries and reference materials?

- What questions are your visitors asking?
- Are there any geographical phrases that are relevant?
- What terminology describes the problems you solve?
- What solutions do you provide?

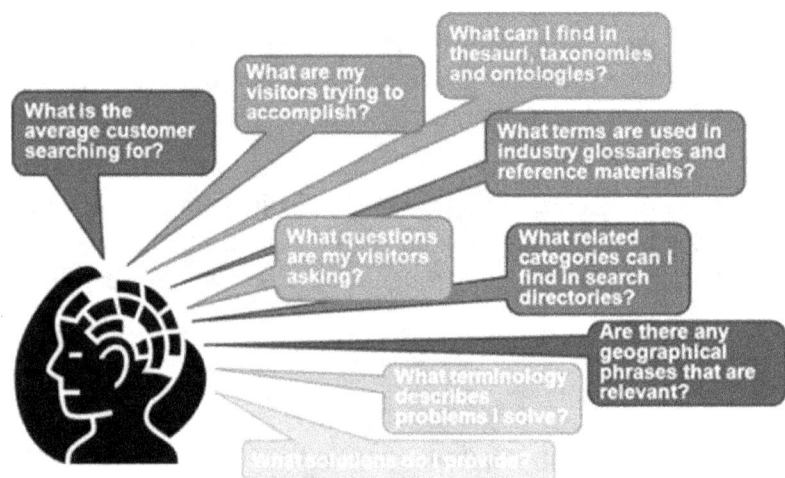

*Illustration by Stoney deGeyter*

**Competitor websites** – In the same way you analyzed your own website, do the same with several of your competitors. Though they may have similar products or services, chances are they describe them a bit differently than you do. Look for alternate ways to describe the same thing. Be careful not to use any trademarked words. Attempting to optimize for those could open a legal can of worms.

**Collection of data** – Analytics data can also provide a wealth of information. If you're set up with Google Search Console or similar tools, you can use these to find search phrases that are currently driving traffic to your site. Bear in mind that this only tells you how people are finding you now and is not necessarily representative of how you want to be found. But culling this data can provide you with additional phrases that you might not have found any other way.

With your list of words gathered from the research above, you're ready to dive into the keyword research tools. Take each word or phrase and plug it into one or more of your favorite keyword tools. Most tools will provide you with lists of related phrases. Many of these you will already have but you're likely to find quite a few that you don't. As you plug in each phrase, you'll eventually reach a point of diminishing returns, receiving results that you've already seen and documented. Once you reach this point, feel free to move on.

Keep in mind that there is no set number of core terms that you're trying to find. Just keep researching until you're confident that you have exhausted all research avenues sufficiently, and that you're unlikely to find anything new or valuable if you keep digging. When you're confident you have a substantially complete list of core terms, you can move on to the next step.

## Step 2: Prioritization

Having a solid list of core terms to work from is a great place to start, but if you've performed exhaustive research, you will probably have more phrases than you know what to do with. This is where prioritization becomes necessary. To effectively prioritize your core terms, you have to look at both the external (has nothing to do with you) and internal (specific to your company) factors.

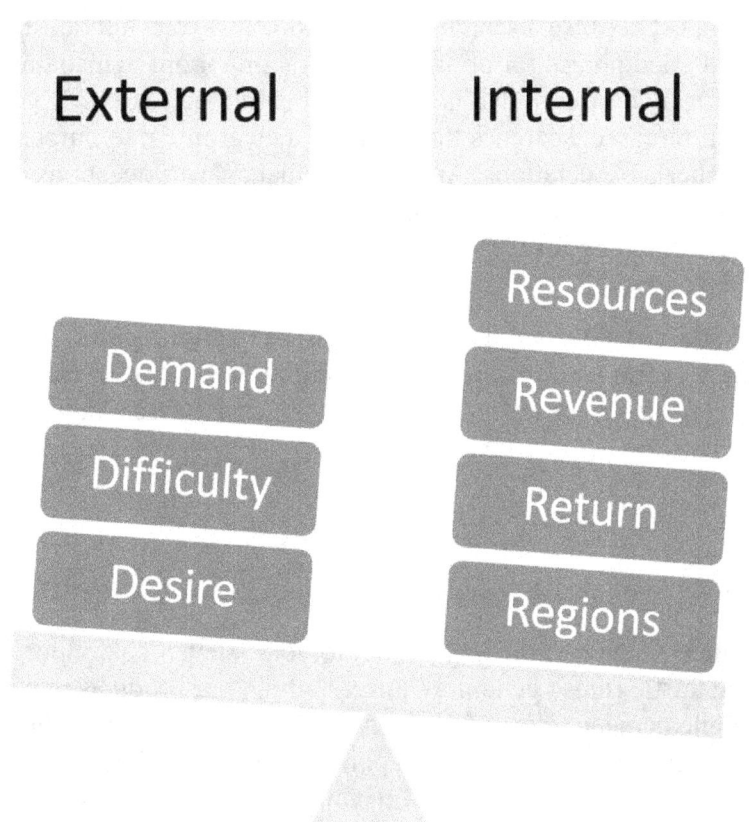

*Illustration by Stoney deGeyter*

## External Factors

**Demand** – Search volume tells you how frequently a core term is searched on a daily, monthly, or yearly basis. This can be an indicator of the actual demand for a particular product or service. Phrases for more frequently searched products may warrant being classified at a higher priority level than phrases with less interest.

**Difficulty** – In addition to search volume, many keyword tools provide a difficulty metric that will tell you how hard it will be to get any given search phrase to rank in relation to the others. The more competition there is for a search phrase, the more difficult it will be to rank, which means more time and resources will be required. While you should never shy away from optimizing phrases that will prove to be hard work, this information can be used to point you in the direction of quicker wins that will provide a more immediate return on investment.

**Desire** – Just because a search phrase is topically relevant doesn't automatically make it a good phrase for optimization. It's important to also understand what the searcher truly desires. What is the intent behind the search? If your site is purely information-based, searches that indicate a clear intent to purchase may not meet the searcher's expectations. And phrases that answer questions are no good for a site that doesn't answer them. Be sure you know what searchers are *really* looking for when searching for any given search phrase, and then prioritize according to what you can offer.

If you have not already, start a spreadsheet to keep all this information organized. It doesn't need to be complex, but you need something you can refer back to frequently. The spreadsheet I use has just five columns: Core Term, Search Volume, Difficulty, Priority, and URL.

## Internal Factors

**Relevance** – Driving traffic (anyone) to your site isn't as important as driving targeted traffic (those genuinely interested in your products or services) to your site. While demand (aka search volume) can be a valuable indicator, the more important factor is how relevant a phrase is to you and the audience you want to draw. Since there are degrees of relevance, it is extremely valuable to rate your core terms accordingly. The more relevant a core term is, the higher it should be prioritized (barring other factors noted here). Less relevant core terms should be set aside for later.

**Resources** – If your workflow or resources are limited, you may not want to dive headfirst into optimizing phrases that could produce more business than you're able to fulfill. Not that you don't want the business, of course, but if some products are hard to restock or are already on frequent backorder, your efforts might be better spent on phrases where you have greater potential to full what the customer requires.

**Revenue** – We all have to keep the lights on. Which means we need to keep the resources pouring in. Prioritize search phrases that will drive traffic to your top-selling products and think about how you might be able to generate even more income by optimizing those product pages. Just because it's already selling well doesn't mean you can't improve on those sales.

**Return** – On the other hand, your greatest profits may not come from your current batch of top-selling products or services. You can often generate the greatest return on investment (ROI) by optimizing phrases based on profit margins rather than current sales and revenue. If you can increase sales of a high-margin product even by a little, this can add a lot to your bottom line.

**Regions** – Different regions of the world often use very different words for the same thing. For instance, depending on where you go in the U.S., there are different words used for carbonated beverages. If your business is localized, rather than national, you'll want to focus on the word variations best suited for your region.

*Illustration by Macey Cave*

When prioritizing core terms, I typically use a sliding scale of 1-10. The result is a list of search phrases that land within each priority level. I find this more helpful than trying to prioritize each search phrase separately.

## Step 3: Core Term/URL Matching

The final step in the Core Term phase is to match up each of your core terms with the appropriate pages on your site. This is a good time (if you haven't done so already) to run a web crawling tool through your site to compile a list of all existing URLs. If you have a large site, it's okay to exclude your blog and other informational pages, for now, focusing solely on primary site pages. Most core terms will fit into the main site anyway.

Before you can attach a core term to a page, there are three things to consider:

**The Point of the Page** – Is the page about travel bags or duffel bags? Or is it about travel bags with wheels? This is where a small nuance in the topic can make all the difference. Be sure that your core term is the absolute best fit for a page, and there are *no other* pages or core terms that work better.

**The Purpose of the Page** – The page's purpose should align with the intent of the core term. You need to deliver exactly what the searcher thinks they'll find when they click into the page. It's not enough to match the desired topic, you must match the overall intent of the search with the content.

**The Proposition of the Page** – Every page has a proposition—a sort of stated goal. What do you want the visitor to do? Make sure the core term you're choosing for the page also aligns with the actions you want your visitors to take and the purpose noted above.

As you begin to match up your core terms and URLs, you might find one URL that is a great fit for more than one core term. In the end, you'll need to pick just one. Using the spreadsheet's sort feature, you can alphabetize your URLs to find the duplicates, then reassess their value to determine which one is best.

It's also possible to find several URLs that could be a good match for the same core term. Again, using what you know about the purpose and goals of the page, you can dig deeper to find the best match.

If your research produced a large number of core terms, you might be tempted to only worry about matching up URLs for the highest priority phrases and then move on to Phase 2. This is risky. More than once I've later found that some of the lower priority core terms were a *better* fit for pages that were optimized for higher priority core terms. If this happens, you'll be forced to re-optimize pages for the better phrase. Getting a full handle on your core terms and pages upfront can save you the hassle of making significant changes later.

When you've completed your URL/core term matching, you will likely end up with more core terms than pages. That's fine. Any core term that doesn't get an assigned URL right now is an opportunity to build new content later.

# Phase II: Discovery Search Phrases

Phase I outlined above can typically be completed in one or two 5-hour sprints and then you're done unless you make major changes to your site offerings. Phase II, however, isn't one-and-done. It's an ongoing process that may take days, months, or even years to refine.

Before we go further, let's refresh ourselves with the difference between how we are defining a core term and a search phrase.

**Core term** – A two (or possibly three) word phrase that represents one of the broader topics a website addresses.

**Search phrase** – A three (or more) word phrase that adds qualifying meaning to a specific core term. This is also often called a keyword or keyphrase in SEO tools.

## What to Look For

To better understand what a search phrase is (and therefore, what a core term isn't), let's look at the five types of search phrases, all built around a single core term:

**Stemmed variation** – Take your core term and transform it using several stemmed endings such as *s, ed, ing, tion, ies*, etc. Using stemmed variations alone, you'll come up with a list similar to the one below for the core term "travel bag." Not every stemmed variation will be relevant, but this gives you the general idea.

- *travel bags*
- *travels bag*
- *travels bags*
- *traveling bag*
- *traveling bags*
- *traveler bag*
- *traveler bags*

**Supplemental modifiers** – Continuing with the *travel bag* core term, you can attach any modifier such as *discount, overseas, wheeled, durable, kids*, etc. to create a pretty long list of highly-relevant phrases. Don't worry about coming up with this list on your own; your keyword research tools will provide this essential information.

- *durable travel bag*
- *discount traveler bag*
- *wheeled traveling bags*

**Stemmed modifiers** – And of course, combining the two above gives you even more search phrases:

- *durable travel bags*
- *travel bag discounts*
- *travel bag with wheels*

**Separated core words** – Keep in mind that any core phrase doesn't have to remain intact to build your search phrase list. It can be any phrase that contains all of the words in the core. Keep in mind that sometimes this may change the intent of the search and no longer be relevant:

- *bags for oversea travels*
- *kids bags for traveling*
- *durable kids traveling bags*
- *traveling with checked bags*
- *how to travel with fewer bags*

**Sphere of influence** – If your business is localized, rather than national, you'll want to focus on the word variations best suited for your area:

- *travel bags in canton ohio*
- *northeast ohio discount travel bags*
- *travel bags near me*

## Step 1: Research Core Terms

Now that you know what a search phrase looks like, you can begin your deep research. There's no doubt that you have vast existing knowledge of your products and services, and you're fully capable of drawing up a solid list of phrases on your own.

However, unless you're in a low-search or niche industry, that approach will likely leave a lot of search phrases (and money!) on the table. For that reason, you should invest in one or more keyword research tools that will help you uncover every potential phrase worth optimizing.

I frequently use more than one tool, as they tend to provide different metrics. By using multiple tools you'll get a better idea of which search phrases are valuable and ensure that you don't leave any undiscovered.

Keep in mind that every keyword research tool works a bit differently. You'll want to pull results that only utilize the words in your core term, rather than "related phrases." If you went through Phase I, you've already gathered related phrases and culled out the valuable core terms. But if you do exact match searches in your tool, be sure to perform a new search for each stemmed variation to uncover every search phrase possible for that core term.

Below is a partial list of the search phrases that my research tool of choice provided. If you look closely, you'll notice that all of the search phrases in this list contain the individual core terms and their stemmed equivalents.

- *travel bag*
- *travel bags*
- *travel bags for men*
- *travel bags for women*
- *travel duffel bags*
- *ohio travel bag*
- *travel toiletry bag*
- *travel makeup bag*
- *best travel bags*
- *walmart travel bags*
- *crossbody bags for travel*
- *car seat travel bag*
- *leather travel bag*

- *mens travel bag*
- *louis vuitton travel bag*
- *golf travel bag*
- *travel cosmetic bags*
- *travel tote bags*
- *travel bag for men*
- *evoc bike travel bag*
- *mens travel toiletry bag*
- *travel bag for women*
- *traveling bags*
- *travel bags target*
- *small travel bags*
- *carry on travel bags*

- *bags for travel*
- *target travel bags*
- *rick steves travel bags*
- *travel luggage bags*
- *womens travel bag*
- *travel bag review*
- *longchamp travel bag*
- *stroller travel bag*
- *mens leather travel bag*
- *hanging travel toiletry bag*
- *best hanging travel toiletry bag*
- *travel bathroom bag*
- *travel cosmetic bag*

The research resulted in over 500 phrases that are actively searched each month. Did you spot the handful of irrelevant phrases in the list above? We'll get to that next.

## Step 2: Analysis and Elimination

You should now have a relatively complete list of search phrases for at least one of your core terms. The next step is to do something with all that data. Before you're ready to start optimizing for your phrases, you have to weed out the junk.

This is one of the more time-consuming steps in the keyword research process because it involves assessing each phrase individually and making sure it is worthy of being included in our final list of search phrases to optimize. But the more time you spend here, the more hassle you'll save later in the keyword research process as well as the on-page optimization.

When deciding what phrases stay and what to eliminate, here are a few things to consider:

**Directly Relevant** – Depending on your core term and industry, you may generate hundreds, if not thousands of phrases from a single core term. Many of these will be irrelevant to your site. The fastest way to sort through this is to search for words that nullify the phrase such as *free*, regions you're not in such as *uk*, or words like *cheap* (unless that is how you refer to your product or service). Also look for brand names of products you don't sell (*walmart, longchamp, evoc,* etc.) and phrases that contain words associated with another core term (*golf, stroller, toiletry,* etc.) This can get tricky because you must decide which word is the subject of the search. In a search for *golf travel bag* is *golf* or *travel* the primary word? These are decisions you'll have to make as you go.

**Desire of Searcher** – Make sure the search phrases represent what the searcher hopes to find on your website. If you don't currently offer what is intended by any phrase, then delete (or set aside) the phrase. With each query, answer the question, "What information does this searcher want?" and "Does the site offer it?" If you're unsure, perform the search yourself. If the results match what you offer, then it's likely a worthwhile phrase. But if the results are for something different, then you may want to delete the search phrase from your list.

**Directioning Upward** – Understanding search trends is important when making decisions on search phrases. Using tools such as Google Trends, you can see the popularity of certain phrases over time. Look for terms that gaining in popular usage. Optimizing for them now will give you an advantage over other sites once those terms become more highly searched.

**Disfavored Volume** – Don't discount low-volume search phrases on that basis alone. Aside from the trends mentioned above, sometimes a search phrase with no measurable search volume can be a perfect phrase to land a high value sale. And some low-volume phrases are ripe for targeting before they start trending. If you can lay claim to a top spot on one of these up-and-coming phrases now, you'll likely have an easier time holding it.

**Dividends** – Determining how much time and effort is needed to get any particular search phrase ranked will give you a good idea of whether it'll be worth your time. In the long run, even the most competitive phrases can be worth the effort, but it's often better for your bottom line to target phrases that will give you a quicker payoff.

Using the list above, you can easily see multiple search phrases that are not relevant to the *Bags! Bags! Bags!* page about travel bags:

- *rick steves travel bags*
- *walmart travel bags*
- *louis vuitton travel bag*
- *evoc bike travel bag*
- *travel bags target*
- *target travel bags*
- *longchamp travel bag*
- *ohio travel bag*

This is obviously just a sampling of the 500+ search phrases found. Even with a solid find/delete technique, you'll need to be prepared to spend a good amount of time sorting through each list. The more irrelevant junk you remove now, the easier the rest of the process will go.

This is also a good time to decide whether or not some phrases should be associated with this or another core term entirely. For example, *Bags! Bags! Bags!* already has pages for duffel bags, car seat/stroller bags, and toiletry/cosmetic bags. Which means we can eliminate the following phrases as they'll come up again when we research out those core terms later:

- *travel duffel bags*
- *stroller travel bag*
- *car seat travel bag*
- *travel toiletry bag*

- *mens travel toiletry bag*
- *hanging travel toiletry bag*
- *best hanging travel toiletry bag*
- *travel bathroom bag*
- *travel makeup bag*
- *travel cosmetic bags*
- *travel cosmetic bag*
- *golf travel bag*

# Step 3: Segmentation into Optimizable Groups

By the time you reach this step, you very well may have whittled your search phrase list down from thousands to hundreds. But due to the sheer volume of what remains, you're no closer to being able to optimize them into your website. This next step will help you properly segment your phrases into smaller, more manageable chunks.

## *Group by secondary core terms*

The first thing you might find is that your list of search phrases can be immediately organized by "secondary core-terms." If we look through my full search phrase list, we'll find several ancillary phrases popping up repeatedly. For example, there are multiple usages of the words *men* and *women*.

### Men

- *travel bags for men*
- *best travel bags for men*
- *mens travel bags*
- *mens travel bags*
- *men's travel bags*

### Women

- *travel bags for women*
- *travel bag for women*
- *womens travel bag*

- *best travel bags for women*
- *travel bag women*

This alone provides two secondary core term groups and a handful of related phrases in each.

Looking further, we can do the same with *wheels/ed* and *roller/ing* phrases. But since the meaning of those qualifiers is the same, we'll keep all of them together into one list rather than creating two separate groups.

## Group by Shopping Intent

The next step of segmenting your phrases is to group them based on where the searcher is in the buying cycle. Because each phase of that cycle requires different content and utilizes different terminology, grouping by intent helps ensure visitors will land on the page that is the best representation of their search.

There are three rough shopping intent groups: Research, Shop, Buy, and one additional group for pure information seekers. (Sorry, I wasn't able to make these alliterative.)

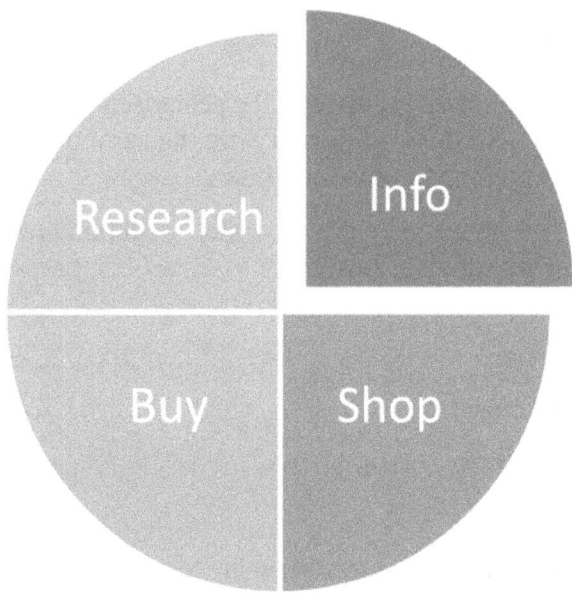

*Illustration by Stoney deGeyter*

**Research** – These searchers are just looking for general information about a product or service. Most likely they are still trying to understand what they want.

Search phrases should be targeted in the higher-level categories of the shopping process.

**Shop** – Searchers in the shop phase have moved into the realm of having intent. They have an idea of what they want; they just don't know the specific details. These search phrases should be targeted on narrower product category pages as well as product comparison pages.

**Buy** – Searchers in this phase have finally narrowed down what they want and are likely ready to move forward on their purchase. They are just looking for the best place to make the purchase. There is no better place to drop these visitors than on the specific product page they are looking for.

**Information** – These are search phrases that are educational focused and may have absolutely nothing to do with making a purchase. They are often "how-to" type searches or are phrased as questions. Essentially, the searcher is looking to gain DIY-type knowledge.

No matter how similar two phrases are, if you determine that the intent between them is different, those phrases should be placed into two separate buckets. This ensures that your optimized pages maintain a singular focus and can effectively meet the searcher's needs.

## Group by Similar Meaning

Now, with your search phrases grouped in the categories above, we can look for those with similar meanings. We did this a bit earlier with the sub-core-term groups, but now we'll dive into similarities based on other qualifiers.

As you look for phrases that can be grouped, start with phrases that have modifiers with meanings. Looking through our master list of *travel bag* phrases, we spot words that have similar meanings:

- *cheap travel bags*
- *bargain travel bags*
- *discount travel bags*
- *travel bags on sale*

All these phrases can easily be optimized on an "on sale" page without diluting the intent or content on the page.

Here's another group of different-but-similar search phrases that we might find:

- *elegant travel bags*

- *designer travel bags*
- *stylish travel bags*
- *luxury travel bags*

*Bags! Bags! Bags!* may not have a page for these phrases now, but we can easily create a page targeting these searches and give the searcher exactly what they want. Keep an eye out for any other phrases that can be grouped in this way.

By grouping phrases according to their meaning, you allow yourself to optimize a single page for dozens of search phrases without having to significantly alter the content. And most importantly, the content's purpose doesn't have to change.

## Step 4: Ensuring Content Viability

One of the most important aspects of organizing your search phrases is to be certain that each phrase in a group can be optimized into a single page without destroying the usability or intent of the page. Never try to force search phrases together that simply are not a good fit. When constructing the page's content, it is important to have a natural flow.

Take a look at the two groups above. A beginner SEO might try to optimize all those phrases into the same *travel bags* page. But as you can see, the search intents are contradictory. It's better to separate the phrases as we did and then optimize them into individual pages. It all comes down to understanding what the searcher is looking for and finding the search phrases that truly fit that search. Grouping phrases that don't work together will make your content awkward and ultimately kill your visitor's experience.

While there is no minimum or maximum number of search phrases you can optimize into a single page, I typically like to have groups of 5-15 phrases. A lot of that also will depend on the content itself. You want to make sure the content can support the phrases without forcing them. In the end, you should have a list that comfortably represents and fits the content on the page.

# Keyword Research Never Stops

This ends the process of researching a core term and grouping the results into tightly optimizable groups. But that was just one core term. From here, you start optimizing pages based on your research results and start researching the next highest priority core term. As I said, it's a never-ending cycle.

In the end, keyword research is more than just another tactic in a successful digital marketing campaign. It's an ongoing process that, frankly, *should* be unending. No matter how thorough you are, you simply won't uncover everything in your first pass. And unless you're in an extremely niche industry with very few relevant search phrases, your opportunity pool is unlikely to dry up anytime soon.

As long as there are search phrases that have yet to be researched and optimized, you have more work to do! As time goes on and new core terms come to mind, or search patterns change, continue to add these new core term ideas to your lists to be researched and optimized at the appropriate time.

Remember, every optimized page is a potential landing page to bring targeted traffic to your site. With a focused keyword research and optimization strategy, you can drive maximum traffic to highly focused pages, getting the best value out of your efforts.

# DOMAIN NAME & URL STRUCTURE

It's commonly assumed that website marketing starts as soon as you have a website. Sounds reasonable. I mean, you can't market and promote what hasn't been built, right?

While this may sound logical, it's far from it. You need to start "marketing" your website long before the first piece of code is written or the first pixel of design is dropped. Waiting is the equivalent of building a house before the foundation is laid.

There's a reason we started this book with keyword research. This is where marketing starts. And, if possible, keyword research should start before you even have a website.

The research performed in the core term research phase can be used to choose the domain name that represents your business. It is also valuable to help map out your website's navigation and architectural structure, as well as the URL structure of your pages.

These are all important considerations before moving forward with website development. Failure to consider them just sets you up for problems down the road. Problems that will be costlier to fix than it would have been to implement correctly from the get-go. Getting out ahead of them will save you thousands of dollars of additional development costs. An underperforming website also results in countless lost sales opportunities.

## Choosing Your Domain Name

If you're just starting a new business, you've probably done a good deal of domain name research. Many of the best domain names are taken, which means you will have to get creative. Unfortunately, this often requires searching through hundreds of domain names just to find some viable options.

Before making your final selection, there are a few guidelines to consider:

- Secure a domain using a .com if possible. Even though other TLDs are becoming more common, people still assume a .com, if they are not sure. If you're not in the US, secure your country's primary Top-Level Domain (TLD). (*.co.uk*, *.ca*, etc.)

- Make sure you own the domain, not your web developer, web host, or Content Management System (CMS) platform.

- Don't use hyphens or strange spellings if you can avoid it.

- Keep it short if possible.
- Use search phrases if possible.
- Ensure it is descriptive and compelling.
- Pick a domain that is easy to remember and easy to say out loud.

■ b-e-a-utiful.com
■ PerfectBeauty.blogspot.com
■ HowToImproveYourImage.com

■ BeautyForMe.com
■ PerfectBeauty.com
■ BeautyIsBeautiful.com

*Illustration by Stoney deGeyter*

Note: capitalization in a domain name is irrelevant. It'll work the same either way.

## Secure Alternate Domain Names

Once you've purchased your perfect domain name (or as near perfect as you can get with what's available), you may want to consider grabbing a few domain variants. You may never use them, but you can protect your brand from poachers. You don't want another company snatching up similar domains in an attempt to capitalize on the brand equity you've been building over the years (known as "cybersquatting").

Alternate domain options to consider:

**Abbreviations -** Think of ways someone might abbreviate your domain name by shortening words. For example, *TheHomeDepot.com* vs. *HomeDepot.com, marketing* vs. *mkg,* or *services* vs *svs.*

**Hyphenation -** As already noted, you don't want a hyphenated domain name for your primary domain, but for brand protection, securing a hyphenated version may be worthwhile. Many businesses do, or will, have similar names to yours, and they may just opt for the hyphenated version despite my warnings against it!

**Alternates and misspellings -** If you tell someone your domain name verbally, there's always the possibility they'll mishear you and spell it wrong. Securing alternate name spellings and misspellings helps you capture traffic from those who type your domain name incorrectly. Want proof? Type gogle.com into your browser and see what happens.

**Brand names -** If you sell a product under brand names different than your company name, it's a good idea to purchase domain names for those as well. You never know when someone will perform a search for your product name and add a *.com* to the end.

**Alternate TLD -** There are so many TLDs now that it's prohibitive to buy them all. But it can never hurt to secure some of the more commonextensions such as .net or .biz, provided you can get them.

Once you secure your alternate domains, be sure to implement a 301 redirect for each. This redirect will make sure anyone trying to find you with that domain will be redirected to the proper one. The chances of these being used by your visitors are small, but you can rest easy that you have done everything you can to protect your brand identity.

# Fix Canonical Issues

Whether you like it or not, your website comes pre-packaged with unwanted duplicate content. We'll address this in detail in a later chapter, but without adding too much duplication here (see what I did there?), we'll briefly discuss one of the universal duplicate content issues here.

By default, every website home page can be accessed with any of the following URLs:

- *http://site.com*
- *http://site.com/*
- *https://site.com*
- *https://site.com/*
- *http://www.site.com*
- *http://www.site.com/*

- *https://www.site.com*
- *https://www.site.com/*

That's eight, and depending on your CMS, there may be four more:

- *http://site.com/index.php* (or .html, .asp, etc.)
- *https://site.com/index.php*
- *http://www.site.com/index.php*
- *https://www.site.com/index.php*

The same goes with each interior page:

- *http://site.com/page*
- *http://site.com/page/*
- *http://site.com/page/index.php*
- *https://site.com/page*
- *https://site.com/page/*
- *https://site.com/page/index.php*
- *http://www.site.com/page*
- *http://www.site.com/page/*
- *http://www.site.com/page/index.php*
- *https://www.site.com/page*
- *https://www.site.com/page/*
- *https://www.site.com/page/index.php*

Multiply that by hundreds or thousands of pages and you've got a lot of duplicate content. If you're not careful, search engines can index each one of these variables separately even though they deliver the same content to your visitors. Left unaddressed, each of these URLs will compete against each other in the search results.

There are three possible solutions here, and like most solutions, some are better than others.

**Solution 1 -** Let the search engines figure it out. Eventually, they do, realizing that each of the variables are the same and treating them accordingly. But there is no guarantee that 1) they will, 2) all link value will be passed to the primary URL, or 3) that they'll select the URL you prefer. And until they "figure it out," you could be competing against yourself.

**Solution 2 -** Add a canonical tag to each URL pointing to the correct one.

*<link rel="canonical" href="https://www.site.com"/>*

This gives the search engines a "signal" that https://*www.site.com* is the version you want them to use for indexing and link valuation. However, the canonical is just a suggestion, and the search engine is still free to reject that suggestion.

**Solution 3 -** Redirect every URL to the "canonical" URL. There are multiple ways to implement these redirects, so talk to your web host or developer, but be sure that every variation 301 redirects back to the canonical version. This is the best solution, because you can maintain complete control over which version of your URL is used by search engines.

## Upper/Lower Case URLs

Another canonical issue that you see from time to time is the use of capitalization in the URLs. Although most modern servers will deliver the same page based on the URLs below, search engines will see them as two separate and duplicate pages.

*www.site.com/Guardians-of-the-Galaxy*

vs.

*www.site.com/guardians-of-the-galaxy*

It's best to stick to always keeping URLs in lowercase.

# Search Engine Friendly URLs

Once you've secured your domain names, you can start planning your website build. But before you jump right into the deep end of the website development pool, there's a lot of background marketing work to hammer out.

Many content management systems don't naturally use search engine friendly URL structures. Far too often, those CMSs produce long and complicated URLs that are hard to type into the browser. Having the ability to customize your URL structure is essential.

A search and user-friendly URL is structured to mimic your website's navigation, using a combination of search phrases, page hierarchy, and brevity.

Example: *www.site.com/category/sub-category/page-name*

If you mapped out your website navigation properly, you will have a strong keyword-rich architecture. Using this architecture for your URLs helps integrate keywords *and* makes your URLs easy to read. This gives the potential visitor a fantastic visual clue as to what the page they are about to visit is about.

Example: *www.site.com/perfume/chanel/allure*

By sight alone, that URL informs the potential visitor that the page in question is about Allure, a perfume by Chanel. This kind of symmetry tells visitors exactly what they need to know before clicking into the page and helps the search engines analyze and rank your content.

## Use Hyphens, Not Underscores in URLs

When building a URL structure that uses multiple words for directory or file names, always be sure to separate the words with hyphens rather than underscores. Historically, search engines have treated words separated by underscores as one word, while words separated by hyphens were treated as multiple words. This may or may not be the case today, depending on the search engine, but from a usability perspective, underscores still tend to be problematic. Hyperlinking the full URL in a web page can make the URL difficult to decipher.

Take a look at these two examples:

*www.site.com/my-dog-ate-my-homework*

vs.

*www.site.com/my_dog_ate_my_homework*

The second URL looks like there are spaces between each word, but they are underscores. The hyphenated one is far easier to interpret. Of course, none of this matters to someone clicking a link, but this is all about eliminating the possibility of error if someone had to type the URL in manually.

## Establish a Proper Hierarchy

There is a common misperception that search engines don't like URLs that are too many directories (also called folders) away from the home page. These folders are represented by the backslash (/). The reality is that search engines don't care how many slashes are in the URL (*www.site.com/page* vs *www.site.com/category1/category2/category3/category4/category5*). They don't even care a whole lot about how many clicks a page is away from the home page, because they know users are likely to enter on multiple pages of your website, not just the home page. What matters most is how your navigation and URLs are organized.

URLs are most effective when they mirror your navigation structure. No matter how you build your navigation, your URLs should follow suit. When in alignment with the navigation, the URL becomes a powerful signal. That means URL structure isn't something that should be decided by the developers, but considered long before development by the marketing team.

There are three types of navigation/URL hierarchy: Flat, deep, and balanced. Like the story of Goldilocks, you want yours to be just right.

## Flat Hierarchy

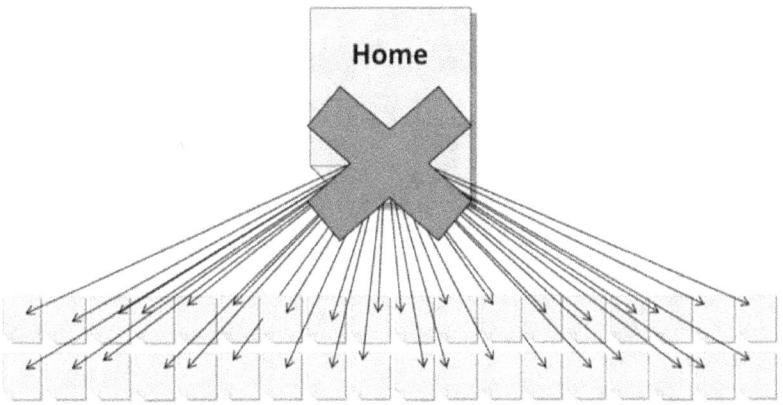

*Illustration by Stoney deGeyter*

Examples:

- *www.site.com/my-dog-ate-my-homework*
- *www.site.com/my-dog-ate-my-proposal*
- *www.site.com/my-cat-ate-my-homework*
- *www.site.com/my-cat-ate-my-proposal*

Notice that each of the "pages" above are placed in a sub-folder residing in the root directory, even though two of them are about "my cat" and two of them are about "my dog." Unfortunately, this has become trendy in some SEO communities due to the common misperception that search engines don't like URLs that are too many folders away from the home page as we discussed above.

Building out a flat navigation is how some SEOs attempt to fool the search engines into believing pages are only a single click from the home page.

Sigh.

Using a flat URL structure effectively kills an important signal search engines use to determine the topic, relevance, value, and weight of a page. The adage, "if everyone is special then nobody is" applies here. A flat structure devalues your most important URLs by making them equal to the least important.

## Deep URL Hierarchy

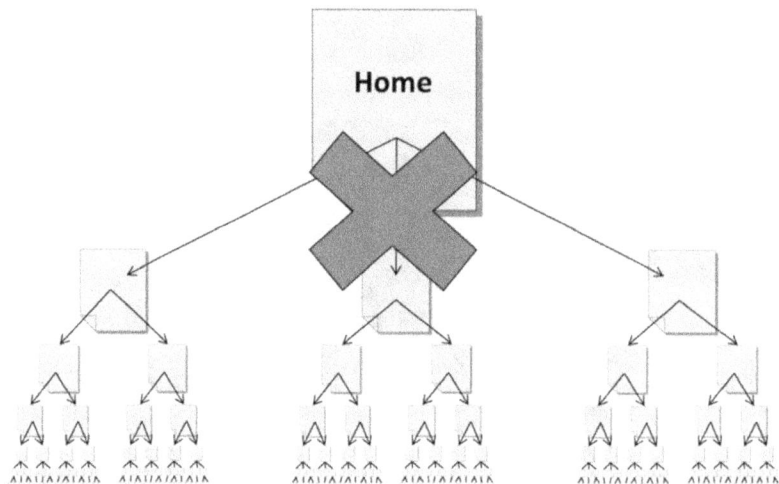

*Illustration by Stoney deGeyter*

Examples:

- *www.site.com/my/dog/ate/my/homework*
- *www.site.com/my/dog/ate/my/proposal*
- *www.site.com/my/cat/ate/my/homework*
- *www.site.com/my/cat/ate/my/proposal*

The opposite of a flat hierarchy is one that is too deep. We noted earlier that search engines don't care how many slashes are in a URL. However, if we look at the URL as a mirror of the navigation, the URLs above tell us that the pages in question are five clicks away from the home page. Is that a problem? Sometimes.

Let's put aside the supposed three-click rule. Most of your content truly should be no more than three clicks from the home page so it's not difficult to find. But there are exceptions, especially with sites with a lot of content that simply doesn't fit neatly within three clicks. Your goal is to make content easy to find. If that's five clicks, then no problem. But there has to be a reason and a method for that.

The problem with deep URL hierarchy is when there is no methodical way to reach the content. It's just all thrown in there willy-nilly. If your content feels buried, search engines will pick up on that. In truth, though, you can have pages ten clicks from the home page and not have them feel buried by linking to these deep pages from other pages that aren't so deep. This gives the search engines a strong URL signal, while also ensuring they find the content more quickly than the URL would suggest.

## The Balanced URL Hierarchy

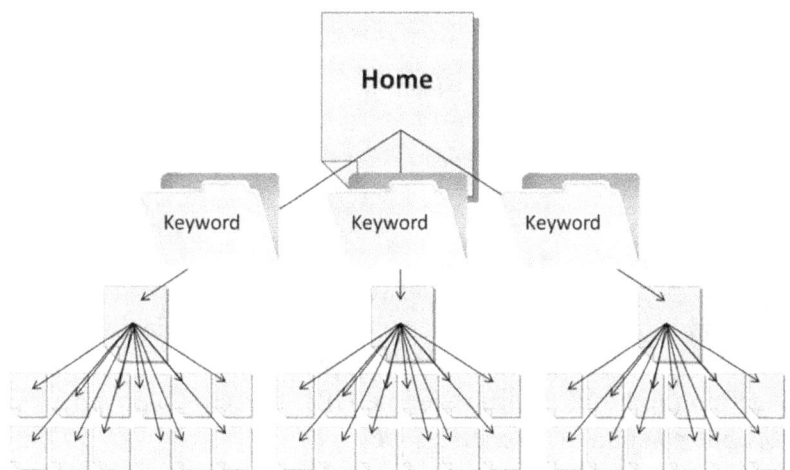

*Illustration by Stoney deGeyter*

Examples:

- *www.site.com/my-dog/ate/my-homework*
- *www.site.com/my-dog/ate/my-proposal*
- *www.site.com/my-cat/ate/my-homework*
- *www.site.com/my-cat/ate/my-proposal*

The perfect URL hierarchy is one that isn't too flat nor too deep. It's "just right." You want each page on your site to be found as quickly as it makes sense to do so. Larger websites are always going to have pages further away from the home page than a smaller sized website, but in the end, it's about making pages easy to get to.

This structure, if mimicking your navigation exactly, gives search engines the highest possible value signals.

# Avoid sub-domains

Sub-domains have a legitimate place for some brands, but for the most part, they are unnecessary and cause more harm than they help. The best-case scenario is that search engines will treat your sub-domain as a sub-folder, but that's not guaranteed. They can also choose to treat a sub-domain as a separate website, which means a lot more marketing work.

Thankfully, it's usually somewhere in between, but even that in-between is not as good as if the sub-domain content was located in a sub-folder.

It's best to avoid using sub-domains except when you want the sub-domained content to be treated as a separate entity from the main site.

> **Bad**: *www.site.com* and *www.mysite.com*
>
> **Better, but not preferable:** *my.site.com*
>
> **Best:** *www.site.com/my*

# URLs Are Important

URL construction is often left to developers or the CMS to decide, but they are an important part of the optimization process. When properly constructed and aligned with your site's navigation (and folder) structure, the URL becomes a powerful signal, not just to search engines but potential customers as well.

Don't let someone else decide the fate of your URLs. Take control of this important signal and ensure every URL is one created by design rather than by chance.

# LINK & NAVIGATION OPTIMIZATION

One of the biggest SEO breakdowns is that far too many websites have poor navigation architecture. On a pure usability level, navigation has one job: get the visitor to the information they need. That may sound simple, but there's a lot under the hood that makes your navigation successful or a complete failure.

Your website's navigation plays a role in usability, findability, search indexing, internal link optimization, and content optimization. All told, navigation provides a framework for a site's structure and contributes to both user and search-friendliness. Get your navigation wrong, and you'll find an otherwise stellar-looking website will perform poorly on multiple key success metrics. Get it right, and you have the foundation to build a high-performance website on all levels.

Let's take a look at the different types of navigation, how they operate, and what good optimization looks like.

## Top Navigation

When it comes to navigation, what is "efficient" for one site may not be efficient for another. Each site is unique and will have unique navigational characteristics. Here are some things that must be considered to determine what is best for your audience.

- Where should your navigation be on the page? Typically, this goes at the top, but it can be centered or justified to the left or right.
- What information needs to be presented in the global navigation?
- How many categories & sub-categories should you include?
- Should you use drop-down (or flyout) menus?
- If space is limited, what navigation items do you include or exclude?
- How do the answers to these questions change for the mobile version of your site?

How you answer these questions starts with understanding the two types of navigation that you'll find at the top of most web pages:

- Primary Navigation
- Utility Navigation

Every site has both of these navigation elements, though sometimes they are combined. But generally, you want to keep these two types of navigation separate visually. As you'll learn below, both types of navigation are essential.

## Primary - Customer Focused Navigation

Your primary navigation is the most visually obvious navigation on the page. This should focus on getting your customers to the product or service information they came looking for. Too many sites use their primary navigation to focus on themselves rather than the customer. Not only does that create a convoluted navigation, but it also makes it difficult for the customer to find the information they need.

If a visitor landed on any page of your site and saw nothing more than the navigation, would they be confident that your site will satisfy their need? If the answer is no, then you have some reworking to do.

Take a look at the two navigation examples below. Both companies are manufacturers, but only one makes what they do clear through their navigation. And the visitor doesn't have to search, read content, or click to figure it out.

#1:

#2:

*Screen captures by Stoney deGeyter*

Now, granted, the page the visitor lands on should let them know if they landed on a site that will meet their needs. But sometimes, even the content isn't that obvious. Especially home page content where you're trying to paint a broad picture. You want your visitors to see quickly that you offer the products or services they came for.

And what if they land on a page that isn't quite what they need? Unless visitors see how to get to the information they want quickly, they'll hit that back button. The more information you can provide at a glance—without forcing the visitor to scroll or click—the better user experience you will provide your visitors.

## Utility - Company Focused Navigation

What about your Contact and About links? Those are important, but not nearly as important as your products or services. Visitors only need that information once they get further into the buying process. Those pages assist with the sale, but you have to show them that you have what they want first.

This leads us to the utility navigation that provides links to your company information. This navigation can still be kept as part of your top nav menu, so it is easily accessible, but keep it visually segmented and less prominent.

Looking at example #2 above, you can see that they place their utility navigation above the primary navigation. It's easy to find, for any visitor that wants that information, but it doesn't distract from the main navigation.

Your company-focused links might vary, depending on what information your visitors need most, but here are some that you should always consider:

**Logo link** – You can add a separate *home* link if you like but always be sure the logo links to the home page.

**About Us** – Visitors may want to learn more about the company.

**Contact Link** – Don't make visitors hunt for a way to get in touch with you.

**Phone Number** – While phone calls are often not preferred by the business, sometimes customers want to talk to someone. Always give the customer what they want.

**Search Bar** – Provide a way to search for your products or information.

**Cart/Login** – Much like a contact link, you want visitors to be able to get to their cart or login to their account easily.

Most well-known brands don't need a prominent about us page, and many companies wish to keep phone calls to a minimum. Adjust the above based on your needs, but only eliminate an option if you're sure you won't lose business by doing so. Also keep in mind that a working phone number can be an important signal of trust if your company brand is not well known.

# Ecommerce Navigation

The challenges for ecommerce websites magnify the importance of establishing a clear and proper navigation structure for your website. Your navigation not only helps your visitors get the content they need, but it also ensures search engines can find and index pages, affording them maximum value in the SERPs (Search Engine Results

Pages). While your primary navigation is important; for ecommerce sites, other navigational options can be equally, or even more important to the overall customer experience.

## Related Products

One of the best opportunities to increase your average sale amount is to add links to additional products that are related to the product currently being viewed. These additional product links can be in the form of similar products, add-ons, or accessories, popular, or even recently viewed items. Any (or all) of these options offer a way to generate additional sales while also adding link equity to those product pages.

Amazon provides a great example of this. In my search for 12 Monkeys (the single greatest sci-fi show in existence), Amazon offers additional products that customers viewed and bought.

*Screen capture from Amazon.com*

Amazon adds over a dozen additional product links using this format. This helps increase the average order value and reinforce the relevant topic for that page.

## Functions vs. Links

Links to other pages on or off your website are an important part of the Internet link graph. Unfortunately, developers often create links that don't go to pages but perform functions on the site instead. Depending on how these links are coded, they can create a loss of page value or cause too many pages to show up in the search index.

Any links that relate to your shopping cart generally should be coded as functions that search engines can't follow. After all, you don't want search engines adding products to your cart. This creates hundreds or thousands of additional pages that simply have no value to searchers.

Other similar function links are product reviews, adding products to wishlists, print this page links, product comparisons, and comments, just to name a few. None of these lead to pages you want indexed so it's better to program these links as functions that are not read as links by the search engines.

In the image below from Best Buy, none of the three buttons/links indicated can be "clicked" by a search engine spider.

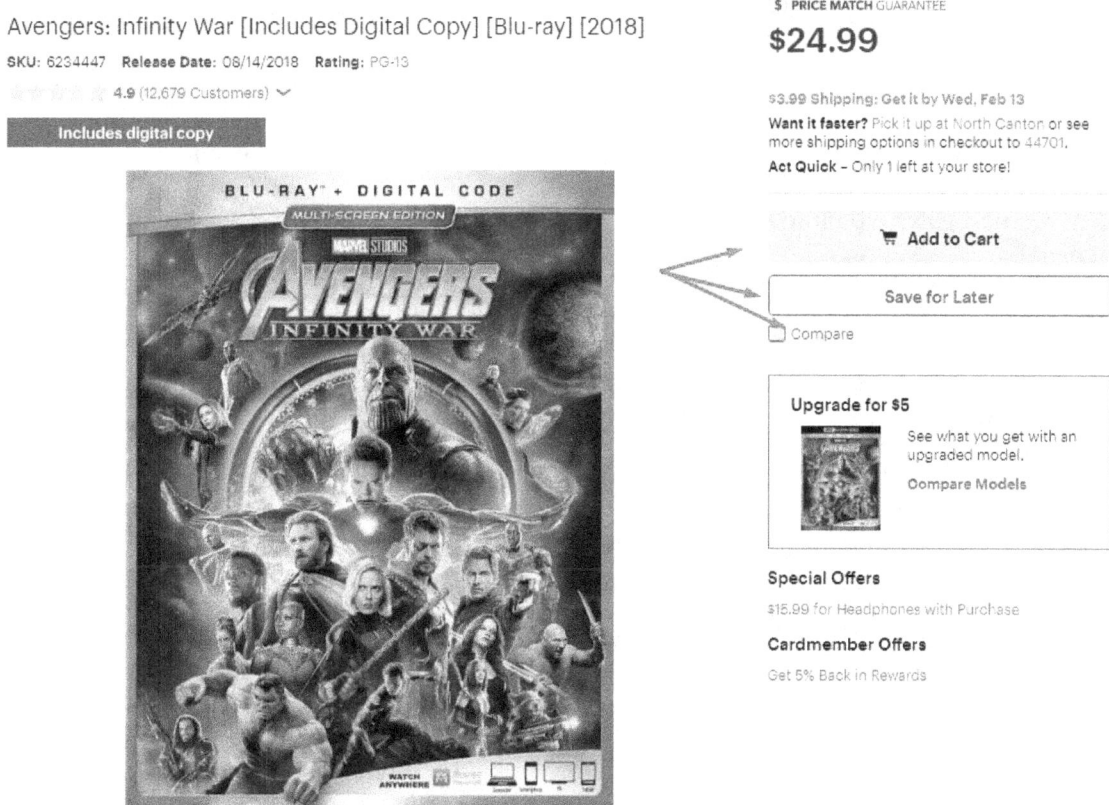

*Screen capture from Amazon.com*

# Filters Vs. Pages

One of the challenges with ecommerce sites is determining when to build indexable pages and when a product filter will suffice.

Let's say you have an apartment finder website and you want visitors to navigate their way to results that fit their living criteria. What's the best way to get a visitor to apartments that fit the following criteria?

- Furnished
- Three-bedroom
- Pet-friendly
- Pool
- Washer and dryer
- Gym
- Utilities included
- Covered parking space

For the most part, you don't need a landing page for each of these options. Many of these options will work quite nicely as filters that simply narrow results on the page. But as a smart SEO, you know that some of those options would also make great landing pages.

To help you decide which of the options to turn into landing pages and which to keep as filters, refer back to your keyword research. If a significant number of people are searching for *3 bedroom apartments*, then that option probably warrants a page with indexable content and a listing of apartments that fit your criteria.

What about the others? Realistically, not as many are searching for a pool, utilities, or a covered parking space. If that hold true for searches in your area, then these options can be filters rather than pages. But if there is any level of search volume that you want to capture, go ahead and create landing pages for those options. There's no sense in missing out on that potential traffic.

## How to Handle Hundreds or Thousands of Products

When it comes to managing the internal link structure of your ecommerce website, you have an especially difficult challenge if you have hundreds or thousands of products. You must provide multiple avenues for shoppers to find your products without creating duplicate content or creating endless loops of filtering options.

Filters are necessary to help shoppers drill down to find the product that best meets their needs. The problem, from a search engine perspective, is they can cause an endless loop of options. This can create thousands of URLs that have little or no differences among them.

Since you already worked out which options need to be structured as filters and which need to have their own landing pages, the rest comes down to programming. Filters should work as functions rather than as links. That alone will spare you a lot of problems.

One thing you might have to do, however, is to create separate filters and landing pages for the same option. For example, say someone lands on the 3-bedroom page. From here, every other option is a filter. But if someone lands on the landing page for furnished apartments, you still need to provide the option for them to filter out all but the three-bedroom apartments they are looking for.

In your navigation, you can link to each of the landing pages, but each of those options will be filters in the other options. This covers all your bases, giving you landing pages where needed, but making sure visitors can filter products down to whatever degree they need.

Before we leave the topic of pages versus filters, your filters must not generate new URLs. If you want to give visitors the ability to bookmark their filtered pages, you'll want to add the filter parameters onto the end of the URL after a pound/hashtag symbol (#). This ensures the search engines don't index the visitor created filtered URLs.

# Other Navigation Types

We've covered the two most important navigations on your website. Now let's take a look at the lesser-but-still-important navigations.

## Breadcrumbs

Breadcrumbs are a website's equivalent of Google's "I'm Feeling Lucky" button. It's used by about 1% of searchers, but most people don't want to see it to go away.

*Screen capture from Google.com*

Breadcrumbs can be a great navigational tool that help both visitors and search engines easily navigate back to higher levels of your website. But their most beneficial usage is that of a visual aid to helps visitors know where they are in the site structure. Breadcrumbs are an at-a-glance indicator that lets visitors see what section and sub-section of the site they are in. And, of course, they can use it to quickly navigate back a step or two.

Home > Men's Clothing > Men's Tops > **Men's Tees & Tank Tops**

Despite their minimal use as a navigation tool, breadcrumbs provide a powerful SEO signal. When your breadcrumb links align textually with your main navigation and URLs, Google will use that as an enhanced signal for understanding a page in relation to the rest of the site. And if you use breadcrumb schema, Google may use your breadcrumb trail in place of the URL in search results.

## Internal Search

There is no substitute for a properly built primary navigation to ensure your visitors can find the information they seek quickly and easily. As noted previously, your primary navigation should do this with as few clicks as possible. But not everyone finds things the same way. Some will work their way through the navigation and others will go directly to your internal site search. And the larger the site, the more likely visitors will be to use search to find what they want.

Your internal search is a valuable tool only if it produces valuable results. If a visitor can't find what they are looking for after performing a search, they'll leave, assuming you don't have it—even if you do. This makes internal site search a potential double-edged sword. It has to work 100% of the time to keep visitors on your site.

As part of your regular site analytics reviews, spend some time analyzing search results from your site. Look at your search logs and start with the most frequently searched phrases. Some things you'll want to consider:

- Are the results accurate?
- Are they helpful?
- Does it lead to the right content mostof the time?
- Is it producing "no results" even when it should?

If you find that your site search isn't producing satisfactory results, you may want to consider removing it from your site altogether. You're better off not having this option than frustrating your visitors with inaccurate or unhelpful results.

One final note, you'll want to make sure that your search results pages cannot be found or indexed by search engines. Search engines have been known to grab search URLs just by watching visitor behaviors. If you keep your search results out of the search engines, you ensure that they spend their time crawling and indexing more valuable pages.

## Footer Menus

Let's start this section off by saying something many people don't want to hear. Your footer is not the place to duplicate your entire top navigation. But that's not to say that it isn't a place for navigation. In fact, the footer is often the go-to place for certain types of navigational options, but not necessarily the ones they can easily find in the main navigation.

Footer navigation serves different needs for different sites. Small sites don't need much more than a link to the privacy policy or a sitemap. Larger sites will want links to shipping or return policies, contact info, or more information about your company.

Use your footer navigation strategically. Place links there that you don't want or need cluttering up the primary navigation. Most visitors won't make it that far down the page, but if they do, it's likely for a reason. Think of your footer as your last-ditch help option. You're not helping visitors find what they already know about, you're helping them get to that harder-to-find but still important information.

## Sitemaps

Site maps provide a way for search engines and visitors to quickly access anything on your site. It's like a shortcut to finding content fast and easy. There are two types of sitemaps and both have value in your ongoing optimization efforts.

### XML Sitemaps

XML sitemaps are commonly used as part of the SEO piece of your digital marketing strategy. As a non-user-friendly file, they provide a way to collect and submit all your pages to the search engine at once.

Since a single XML sitemap file can contain up to 50,000 links, most sites only need one. But if you like, you can create separate sitemaps for different types of pages (i.e. products, blogs, images, etc.).This isn't strictly necessary until you have over 50k links or the sitemap is larger than 10MB.

You can link to your XML sitemap in your robots.txt file with a single entry:

*Sitemap: https://www.site.com/sitemap.xml*

You'll want to be sure to keep it updated whenever your pages change. And don't include non-canonical URLs, thank you pages, or any other URL that you don't want search engines to find.

## *HTML Sitemaps*

An HTML sitemap is one that is developed primarily for your site visitors. It's a one-stop-shop for visitors to find any page on your site quickly, provided the sitemap is updated and organized in a user-friendly way.

HTML sitemaps are becoming increasingly rare but they can be a valuable tool for sites that have deep content. As a proponent of having a balanced site architecture, you might think I'd be against HTML sitemaps as they flatten how the architecture is understood. But search engines understand the difference between your main navigation and a sitemap and treat them accordingly. In short, HTML sitemaps don't harm your architecture in any way.

Be sure to keep your HTML sitemap organized and updated as your site changes. If it's nothing but a collection of unorganized links or if a lot of the links redirect or return a 404 Not Found status error, you might as well forgo it and focus on your XML sitemap instead.

# Negative Navigation Designs

Having a strong navigation isn't just about having the right information in the right place, you also need to present that information in the right way.

Up to this point, we've focused on navigation elements your site needs. But now let's address a couple of navigation design elements that are somewhat counterproductive for good SEO.

There are innumerable ways to design a good navigation menu, but only a couple of things you should avoid.

# Mega Menus

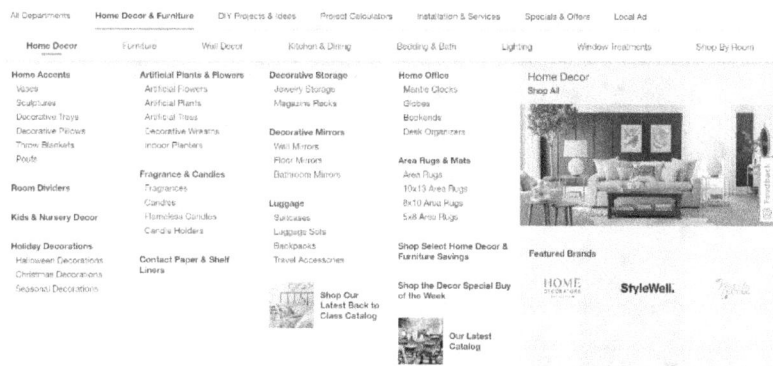

*Screen capture by Stoney deGeyter*

There's been a recent move by the design and development community to cram as many links as possible into a website's navigation. The theory behind this is to create a few clicks as possible to find the content. While I won't argue with the intent, it's the execution I have a problem with. And it often comes with its own set of unintended consequences.

The problem with mega menus is that it eliminates all aspects of hierarchy and it essentially creates a flat site structure. The intended hierarchy may be obvious visually, but it's non-existent to the search engines.

But even worse, mega menus create far too many options for the visitor. Options are good, yes, but too many leads to decision paralysis. Visitors can't process that much info in a short amount of time and they end up clicking on whatever option they see first, which usually isn't what they really want.

At any point, your navigation should only provide seven or eight options at most. By keeping the options minimal, visitors are better able to digest the options and make a decision that is more likely to lead them to the information they want.

The additional benefit of properly segmented menus is that they get the visitor to take action. Once they commit one action, it's easier to get them to commit to the next, provided you do a good job of leading them toward better content.

## Drop-Down Menus

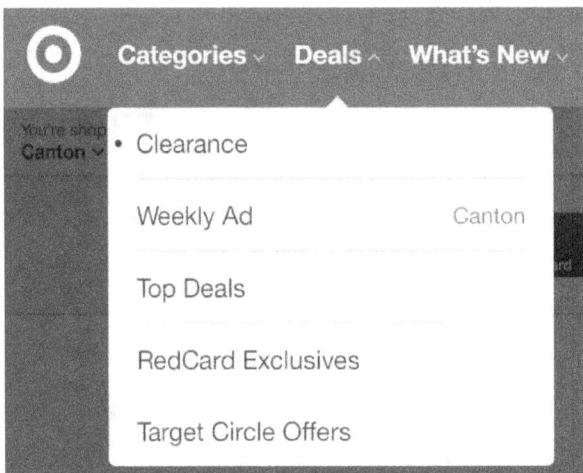

*Screen capture from Target.com*

The little brother of the mega menu is the drop-down menu. I'm not 100% opposed to using them as they do a better job of leading the visitor to content, but they still have the issue of flattening the architecture. That alone makes drop-down menus unappealing to me. The additional problem with drop down menus is that they do not perform well on mobile, because on mobile, there's no such thing as a mouseover.

Again, going back to what we discussed above, it's preferable to lead the visitor on the journey, one click at a time.

## Flyout Menus

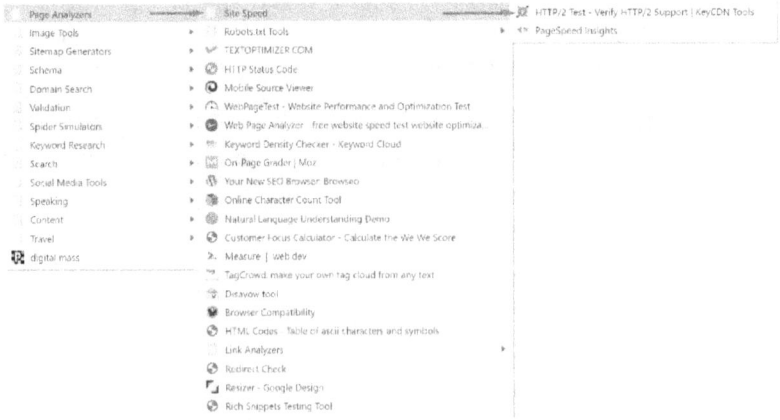

*Screen capture by Stoney deGeyter*

If there is one type of menu I despise more than all others it's the flyout menu. Flyout menus have all the negative issues of the drop-down, but if you're not careful, they add a whole lot of usability problems as well.

With a drop-down menu, you generally have a hundred horizontal pixels or more for your mouse pointer to stay on track with the menu. But with a flyout, the menu path is thinner horizontally for the side-to-side mouse movement. Far too often the mouse cursor moves outside of that narrow window, causing the menu to collapse before you make your selection. At times, it seems like you need surgical precision to stay on track to click the link you want. As mentioned above, the flyout menu doesn't function at all in mobile either.

Mouse movement issues can be fixed by adding time delays before closing the menu, but you're just fixing one problem so you can keep the others.

# Optimization Considerations

As part of the SEO industry, when we hear the term "optimization" we often think of "search optimization." (This is why I prefer the term "web presence optimization" over "search engine optimization." We don't optimize search engines but rather the entirety of a business' web presence. Okay, I'll jump off my soapbox now.) An important part of optimizing a website is to optimize it for visitors. Both search engines and visitors are important. Search engines understand this, and they don't want to direct their users to websites that won't serve their needs. Google in particular keeps adding elements of user experience to how they determine site rankings.

Most of the optimization considerations below lean more heavily in the search or visitor direction, but most will hold some value for both.

## Keywords in Link Text

Your website's navigation is one of the easiest places to get keywords into links. After all, if you're presenting a link to your Coat Racks page, you're not going to put "That thing you hang your coats on" in your navigation. But navigation isn't the only way to help visitors find relevant content.

I like to think of a site's navigation as a back-up system. The best way to get visitors to the content they need is through the content itself, and more specifically, links in your content to relevant pages. Content-based links are one the best ways to keep visitors engaged with your site.

Just like in your navigation, using relevant keywords in your text links is important. Instead of, "Click here to learn more about preparing personal tax returns," a better way to link would be, "Learn more about preparing personal tax returns." If the visitor or search engine considers nothing but the link text, it's the second one that informs them what will happen when they click.

It's always a good idea if you can work your call to action into the link. In which case you'd have a more robust link: Learn more about preparing personal tax returns. This option includes both the relevant keywords and the call to action. It also helps prevent obvious over-optimization, which can cause a search engine red flag.

## Related Topics

A close cousin to adding links to related products in your ecommerce site is linking to related articles on your blog. Adding a handful of additional links to related posts is another great way to share link love to those pages and keep visitors engaged on your site for a little additional reading.

Now read this:

- Go Blog Yourself: Writing Your Blog Posts with Pen in Hand and SEO In Mind
- Write for The Three Types of Readers
- Why We Write, and How You Learn
- Go Blog Yourself Step 8: Do It Right and Do It Again
- Go Blog Yourself Step 2: Know What They Want To See

*Screen capture from PolePositionMarketing.com*

Just make sure that if you include "related links," they are actually related! Poorly related content can be the death of good topical relevance.

## HREF Linking

Unless you're purposely trying to block search engines from reaching certain pages of content, you'll want to use only spiderable (crawlable) HREF links. Search engines have gotten pretty good about following all kinds of non-HREF links, but they are still not perfect. So while you can get away with other forms of links but there is always the risk that Google won't follow or weight the link properly.

Any HREF link is guaranteed to be read and followed by the search engines unless you tag it with a *nofollow* attribute (see next section). This is the surest way to have your links followed and pages indexed.

> *<a href="http://www.site.com/category/sub-category/page.htm">Link Text Goes Here</a>*

Other types of links can be problematic:

> *javascript:plnav('h09264','pl','image')*
>
> or
>
> *JavaScript:window.open('http://www.site.com/category/sub-category/page.htm', 'newWindow')*

In the two examples directly above, one of them contains a URL. This one is far more likely to be spidered and given correct attribution. The other is anyone's guess.

Another common way to deliver traffic to content is to use form selectors. Again, this is a hit and miss situation. You may get the visitor where they want to go but you may very well be hiding the pages from search engines. If a page is important, stick to using search engine-friendly HREF links across the board.

## Static (Absolute) vs. Dynamic (Relative) URLs

There are two types of internal links: Static and dynamic (also referred to as absolute and relative links). Static links contain the full URL in the HTML code, and dynamic links contain only what is relevant to get the visitor to the page being linked to.

> Static: *https://www.site.com/the-dog-at-my-homework*

> Dynamic: *../the-dog-ate-my-homework*

Dynamic URLs require the browser to interpret the link destination based on where the linking page resides in relation to another or for the developer to use a base href command. This means there's room for error. Moving a page or copying content from one page to another page will often break the link. In the worst case scenario, using dynamic links can create duplicate content, because as the user moves from one wrong link to another, the duplicate URLs increase.

Static links leave no room for interpretation. The link points exactly where you want the visitor to go.

The only downside to using static links is if the linked page location changes. You'll need to make sure all static links are updated as well.

# Blocking Pages from Being Indexed

As mentioned earlier, there are times when you may not want pages to show up in search. There are a few options for blocking those pages, each with their own set of pros and cons. You'll have to decide which option to go with depending on the end goal of keeping any particular page out of the index.

## Robots.txt File

The robots.txt file is your "master control" for telling the search engines what pages to or not to crawl. When search engines first visit your site, they look for and download this file. This provides instructions for what they can or can't do on your website.

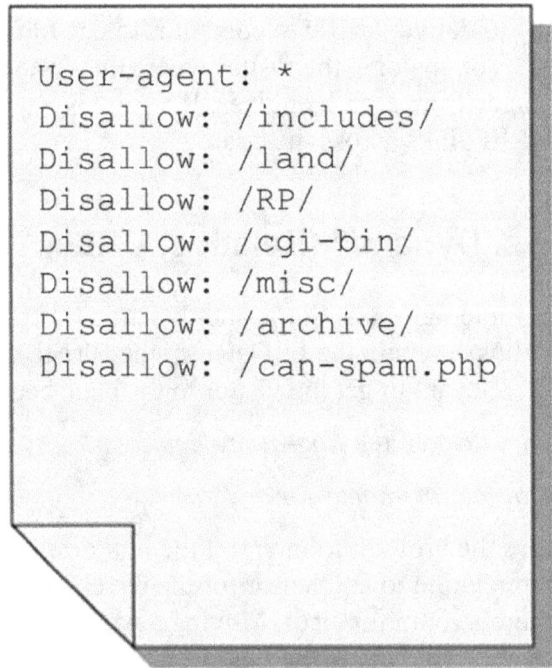

```
User-agent: *
Disallow: /includes/
Disallow: /land/
Disallow: /RP/
Disallow: /cgi-bin/
Disallow: /misc/
Disallow: /archive/
Disallow: /can-spam.php
```

*Illustration by Stoney deGeyter*

As you can see from the example above, the robots.txt file is rather simple. At the same time, if you mess this up you can wreak havoc on your website when it comes to search engines.

The primary purpose of the file is to let search engines know what pages (or folders) you want them to stay out of. This means you must be sure you don't inadvertently disallow pages that you want visitors to find.

There are plenty of tutorials written to help you craft the robots.txt file specific to your needs, including allowing or disallowing certain search engines. But I cannot stress enough the importance of getting this page right. One wrong move can wipe out all your search engine rankings almost instantly.

Also, be aware that while this will tell the search engines not to crawl the page, but it won't prevent the page from showing up in search results. Google won't read or analyze the content of the page, but through other signals such as links, disallowed pages can still show up in search results.

## NoFollow, Sponsored, and UGC Link Attributes

A *nofollow* attribute can be added to any link on your website. Originally designed as a vote of no confidence to the page you're linking to, it was a way to tell Google not to give any link credit to the page. Over the years the function and purpose of the *nofollow* has evolved. Google made it a requirement on all ads or paid links, and more recently they downgraded it as merely a signal rather than a directive.

> *<a rel="nofollow" href="http://www.site.com/category/sub-category/page.htm"></a>*

More recently, Google has rolled out two new link attributes, *sponsored* for ads, and *ugc* for user-generated content links.

> *<a rel="sponsored" href="http://www.site.com/category/sub-category/page.htm"></a>*

> *<a rel="ugc" href="http://www.site.com/category/sub-category/page.htm"></a>*

Google has stated that these are merely hints for the algorithm to consider when determining the value of the linked pages. For the most part, they don't care which directive you use, but I won't be surprised if the *nofollow* is phased out in a decade.

Because these are only hints, these link attributes are no longer a viable way to keep search engines from indexing the content.

## Robots Meta Tag

Your best option to keep pages from showing up in search is to add a robots meta tag with a *noindex* directive.

*<meta name="robots" content="noindex">*

When search engines crawl the page, this directive prevents them from including the page in the index, which keeps it out of the search results completely. If this tag is added to a page already in the index, it will be removed the next time the page is crawled.

Even though this is the best way to keep content out of the search index, it does have its downsides. Namely, the search engines have to spider the page before they can receive the instructions not to index it. If you have a lot of these pages, then the search engine will use up resources spidering these pages even though you'd probably prefer they don't. This can consume valuable crawl budget. Another thing to keep in mind is that just because a page won't be indexed, doesn't mean it can't be crawled and the links on that page followed.

In a way, the robots meta tag works opposite of the robots.txt file. Where the file keeps crawlers away from the page but not out of the index, the robots *noindex* meta tag will keep the page out of the index but not prevent it from being crawled. And unfortunately, the two don't play together well.

If you use the robots.txt to disallow the page, you can't also tell the search engine to keep it out of the index because they'll never read the meta tag. Which means the best option for excluding content is the meta tag. And if you don't want any of the links on the page to be followed, be sure to add a *nofollow* attribute to the meta tag as well.

*<meta name="robots" content="noindex,nofollow">*

But again, this is only used as a hint, not a directive.


# Redirecting Moved or Removed Pages

An ongoing problem with the web, in general, is that pages are constantly being moved or removed from websites. Sites go defunct, rearrange their site structure during a new site build, or just delete old content that is no longer relevant. When this happens, there is a good chance that a link or bookmark to those moved or removed pages is no longer valid.

When this happens, you can either allow the visitor to receive a "page not found" notice, or redirect them to another page. Let's discuss both options.

## Page Not Found

There are two types of page not found error messages. The default message might look something like this:

# Not Found

The requested URL /404/ was not found on this server.

*Screen capture by Stoney deGeyter*

Or a customized one might look like this one from LEGO.com:

*Screen Captaure from Lego.com*

If you're wondering which of the two options is better, let me save you the time. The second. Visitors who hit the first page are more than likely to hit the back button and find another option on their journey. Visitors who land on the second are likely to hit that "start shopping" button.

But you can customize yours however you want. Maybe give them a few of your most popular options. The goal here is to keep the visitor engaged with the site rather than stopping them in their tracks.

Needless to say, however, even a customized broken link page isn't optimal. In most situations, you want to redirect the old URLs to the current location of the content, or its nearest current counterpart.

## Redirected URLs

Whenever a page is moved (or the URL is changed) you should implement a redirect from the old URL to the new one. This ensures that anyone visiting that old URL through a link or bookmark of some kind will automatically land at the page's new location. They'll likely be none the wiser that the URL changed, and that's what you want. They don't need to be aware of your housekeeping issues.

On the search engine side, the redirect serves as a way to tell the search engines to transfer all "value" of the page from the old URL to the new one. This helps maintain most, if not all, of the link equity built up on URLs that no longer work. That's a win-win.

Not every page is a candidate for redirection in the truest sense. Let's say you sell widgets and thingamajigs. But you decide that widgets are not profitable so you stop selling them to focus on thingamajigs. Since there are no more widget pages on your website, there is no proper location to redirect that old content to. Some people suggest you can let traffic to those old URLs hit a 404 Not Found message.

I'm not a fan of this approach. It's better to redirect the visitor to a landing page with a message that you no longer sell widgets but that they may be interested in thingamajigs. At the very least, this will help maintain your link equity on the removed pages, and at best, it gives your visitors a reason to stick around.

So, if every moved and removed URL gets redirected, is there still a need for a 404 page? Yes, absolutely. You never know when someone might delete or change a URL and not set up the appropriate redirect. This at least gives the visitors a fallback. If you scan your site regularly for broken links, these changes will show up and then you can set up your redirect.

# Navigation is No Trifling Matter

Your website's navigation and link structure are the backbones of your entire website. They play a critical role in how easily your visitors find the information they need and give the search engines much-needed indicators of content and its relative importance to the rest of the website.

When first taking on a website optimization project, after addressing any three-alarm fires uncovered in early analysis, the site's navigation is one of the first things to address.

Unfortunately, changing a site's navigation and URL structure is no easy task and can take months to plan and execute. But it's worthwhile and is a significant contributing factor to the success or failure of your website, both from a search and user experience perspective.

# TITLE TAG OPTIMIZATION

When it comes to on-page optimization, a web page's title tag is the single most important piece of optimizable real estate. Think of it as the beach-front property of SEO where space is extremely limited and you must use it wisely. Compared to other optimizable parts of a page, the title tag holds the greatest per-pixel impact due to it being extremely limited in space and exceptionally powerful in SERPs. Aside from the website's entire architecture, I can't think of any single area of a site that holds as much power to sway search engine rankings and clicks as the title tag.

## What is a Title Tag?

Every webpage has a snippet of code called a title. This is not visible on the page itself but can be seen by searchers and website visitors in other ways. (We'll get to that later.) The general idea of a title is to act as a one-line description of what visitors can expect when they land on the page. Think of it as a title for a college paper or business report. It should act as a short, compelling introduction that entices the readers to read more.

Title tags must be placed in the <head> section of the page's code to be properly interpreted and displayed:

*<head>*

*<title></title>*

*</head>*

And the actual title is found between the opening and closing title element:

*<title>This Is Your Page Title</title>*

## How and Where is the Title Tag Displayed?

There are four places where visitors are likely to see a page's title tag. Each of these will have varying degrees of impact on your audience.

## Search Engine Results Pages (SERPs)

Whenever a search is performed, Google and other search engines often use a page's title tag as the clickable link in the results. This is what most people see, scan, and read as they are deciding which site to visit after a search. In the image below, the purple text comes straight from the title tag.

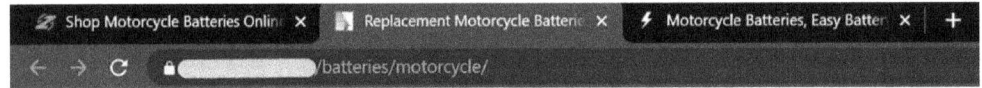

*Screen capture from Google.com*

## Browser Tabs

Desktop web users frequently have multiple browser tabs open at a time. It may be three, a dozen, or more. The first 1-3 words of your title will show in the tab, depending on how many other tabs are open. Keep this in mind when crafting your page titles. Put the most important information in front.

*Screen capture by Stoney deGeyter*

## Browser Bookmarks

If (or hopefully when) a visitor bookmarks one of your pages, the default bookmark text will be the page's title. Just as with the search results, your bookmarked page will be competing against other sites the visitor has bookmarked. You want to make sure your title tag stands out from the rest. (Note: The text of the bookmark can be edited by the user, but it's rarely done).

Shop Motorcycle Batteries Online -

Replacement Motorcycle Batteries - Order A Motorcycle Battery

Motorcycle Batteries, Easy Battery Finder |

*Screen capture by Stoney deGeyter*

## Social Links

When pushing content to social media channels, if you have not set a separate social title, any shared content will feature the page's title tag. If it's too long or uses unnecessary words, this may create a not-so-compelling or click-worthy title. For maximum social value as well as search, your title tags need to compel a click. Because what is compelling varies, you can always try different titles to see what generates the most traffic and engagement.

# Benefits of a Well-Constructed Title Tag

Despite being such a small part of a complete optimization strategy, a title tag delivers big results, impacting search, usability, and social media. If you could make only one change to a page for search engine ranking purposes, it should be the title tag. Here's why:

## Titles Influence Rankings

Adding or moving keywords in a title tag can mean the difference between a page not ranking at all and one that ranks on the first page in the SERPs. Results vary depending on competition and other factors, but I've seen pages move up several pages simply by updating the title tag to include relevant keywords.

## A Good Title Persuade the Click

Since the title tag is (usually) displayed in the search results or on social sites, it is often the very first point of influence that entices someone to click into your site. If your title isn't compelling, then all your top rankings and social shares ultimately won't amount to much, as potential visitors bypass it for more compelling options. Chances are, the one you *did* click on was the most compelling of the batch.

## The Title Increases Visibility

When looking for social engagement, the more compelling your title, the greater likelihood the post will be shared and passed along by your followers. Regardless of how great your content is, boring titles will get skimmed and passed over. Exciting titles, however, engage the audience to both click and share. The better your title, the more engagement and better visibility your page will have.

# How to Craft a Successful Title Tag

Despite its small footprint, crafting a successful title tag isn't always easy. Every display platform has differing limitations and serves a different purpose. This makes careful consideration of your tag essential. Poorly crafted and structured words will be skimmed over at best, and at worst demonstrate incompetence. Using effective writing and optimization practices will ensure your title tags are worthy of the attention you want them to receive.

## 50-60 Character Limit

While there is no maximum length for a title tag, there are limitations to what will display in any given platform. The primary standard to use is what searchers see in Google search results pages. Google displays about the first 600 pixels of a title tag, but unless you have your pixel ruler handy, this isn't all that helpful. Though character width varies, Google displays up to 60 characters of a title tag on average. That makes a "safe" title tag length between 50-55 characters. After that, you risk part of the tag getting cut off, unseen to the searcher.

To be safe, you should always double-check how Google displays your title tags for at least a handful of important search phrases and pages. If it gets cut off, or Google rewrites it significantly, you may want to tweak it. That said, there is nothing inherently wrong with a long title so long as you are okay with how it looks, and nothing important falls outside of the display area.

The two examples below show the difference in a title that is slightly too long vs. one that is just right.

*Screen capture from Google.com*

Vs

*Screen capture from Google.com*

You'll note that the second title tag fits entirely in the result, while the first one shows that there is more that didn't fit. It's up to you to decide if that's okay or not.

## Use Keywords

Keywords are an important part of both SEO and user experience (UX). People search using certain phrases because that is how they think about the product, service, or information you offer. If you want them to notice your site among the many in the SERPs, your title tag has to be relevant to that search. One way to do that is to use the phrases they search for (keywords) in your title tag.

Of course, you never know what they will be searching for, or what keywords your page might show in the SERPs for, but you do know the overall topic of each page on your site. That information gives you a good idea of what words to use in your title tag. If your title tag lacks keywords, there's a very real possibility that it won't resonate with what the searcher is looking for, even if the page it represents is a strong match.

It's always a good idea to place the keywords as close to the front of the title tag as possible. Here are a few reasons why:

1. It is believed that Google weights information at the front of your title tag more heavily than information toward the end. If you're trying to improve your rankings for a page, sometimes moving the keywords from the middle or end of the title tag to the front can make a difference.
2. Searchers scan down the left side of the page. Placing keywords where they scan increases the odds of the searcher noticing the link to your site and finding it to be relevant.
3. When your page is open in a tab, only the first couple of words might be displayed. If your keywords are not in the front, then the visitor will have a harder time getting back to it and may pass it up for other open tabs.

## Be Compelling

More than anything else, your title tag must compel the reader to click it. If putting keywords in the front destroys readability and click-worthiness, then change it up, even if it sacrifices rankings. A top ranking in the SERPs does nothing if searchers are not clicking because of a poorly written title tag.

# Title Tags for Brand Building

There is an ongoing question of whether the business name belongs in the title tag. With such limited space, one must consider carefully if doing so adds value or simply uses valuable real estate.

For the most part, any non-branded search indicates that the searcher isn't concerned about who's providing the product or service, they are just interested in finding the relevant information.

But that's not to say there isn't value in having a business branded title tag. As searchers perform multiple searches, seeing your business name come up repeatedly—regardless of position in the search results—can produce a branding impact on their decision-making processes.

As a general rule, where and when to add your brand name to your page's title tags depends on what kind of business you are:

**Recognizable Brands -** Place your business name in the front of your title tag when most shoppers will automatically recognize it or if your customers regularly make purchase decisions on brand-name alone.

**Building Brand Recognition -** Place your business name at the tail end of your title tags when you are not a notably recognizable brand but feel that brand recognition within your industry is valuable to build consumer loyalty.

**No Brand concern -** Don't use your business name when your brand name adds no sway in the purchase decision.

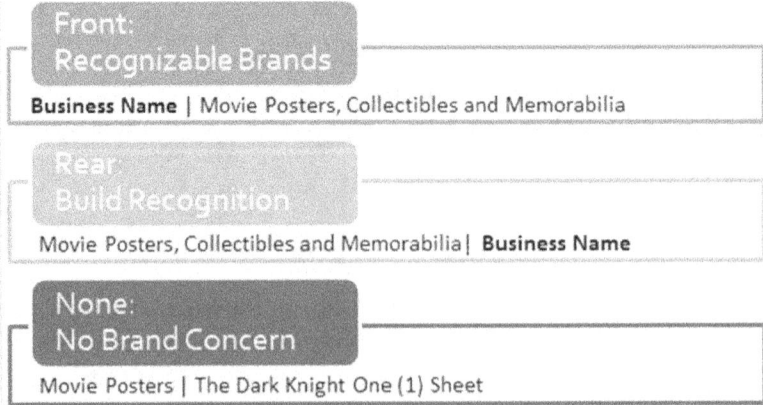

*Illustration by Stoney deGeyter*

Placing your business name in your title tags should always increase the clickability of your site from the search results. If for any reason this prevents you from adding other, more valuable information, it may be best to leave the tag unbranded.

# META TAG OPTIMIZATION

If you were going to tell a "back in the day" story about digital marketing, it would have to include a discussion of meta tags. Long before links were built, before content was king, and before social was sharable, meta tags were optimized. Meta tag optimization is the original SEO.

But the days of throwing long lists of keywords into a meta tag to move your site to the first page of Alta Vista, Excite, or Webcrawler are long gone. For that matter, gone are Alta Vista, Excite, and WebCrawler. But even as today's digital marketing has long surpassed the glory days of SEO being all that mattered, some of these old school optimizations are still relevant to an effective digital strategy today.

## What are Meta Tags?

There are over 25 commonly used meta tags, each serving a unique purpose. Meta tags are located in the <head> section of a page's HTML code. Typically unseen to visitors, meta tags provide information and directives to browsers, social media sites, and search engines.

```
<meta name="keywords" content="your, tags"/>
<meta name="description" content="150 words"/>
<meta name="subject" content="your website's subject">
<meta name="copyright"content="company name">
<meta name="language" content="ES">
<meta name="robots" content="index,follow" />
<meta name="revised" content="Sunday, July 18th, 2010, 5:15 pm" />
<meta name="abstract" content="">
<meta name="topic" content="">
<meta name="summary" content="">
<meta name="Classification" content="Business">
<meta name="author" content="name, email@hotmail.com">
<meta name="designer" content="">
<meta name="copyright" content="">
<meta name="reply-to" content="email@hotmail.com">
<meta name="owner" content="">
<meta name="url" content="http://www.websiteaddrress.com">
<meta name="identifier-URL" content="http://www.websiteaddress.com">
<meta name="directory" content="submission">
<meta name="category" content="">
<meta name="coverage" content="Worldwide">
<meta name="distribution" content="Global">
<meta name="rating" content="General">
<meta name="revisit-after" content="7 days">
<meta http-equiv="Expires" content="0">
<meta http-equiv="Pragma" content="no-cache">
<meta http-equiv="Cache-Control" content="no-cache">
```

*Screen capture by Stoney deGeyter*

Though not technically a meta tag, you'll often hear a page's title tag referred to as such. Since the title tag's importance towers over all other meta tags, it merits a chapter of its own. So, in this chapter, we'll cover the remaining few meta tags that are important to digital marketing. Let's start with the lesser important tags and end with the Grand Poobah: The Meta Description.

# Keyword Meta Tag

*<meta name="keywords" content="you, can, put, your, keywords, here, but, you, really, shouldn't, bother" />*

The meta keyword tag is largely irrelevant to modern search engines. None of the major search engines use the keyword tag as a ranking signal. At best, some internal search applications will use the meta keyword tag to determine how to rank your pages, but that's about it. This tag can be ignored.

# Content-Type Meta Tag

*<meta http-equiv="Content-Type" content="text/html; charset=utf-8" />*

The meta *content-type* tag allows you to specify the media type and character set for the page. This helps the browser know how to render the code. While the tag itself is completely meaningless to the visitor, it can impact how visitors see the web page. Entering the wrong *content-type* can impact the visitor's on-page experience.

# Viewport Meta Tag

*<meta name="viewport" content="width=device-width, initial-scale=1">*

Similar to the content type, the viewport tells the browser how the page content should be displayed. This is especially important in a world where visitors use multiple device types and screen resolutions.

Both the content type and viewport meta tags are pretty standard and will likely be the same on every page. Once your developer sets those, you won't have to think about them until the next site redesign.

# Robots Meta Tag

*<meta name="robots" content="noindex, follow">*

The robots meta tag is used to set indexing control parameters for the page. It's not an essential tag for every page, but when used, it becomes an essential tag to instruct search engines about what they can or cannot do with your content.

Below is a list of the various parameters that can be added to the content portion of the meta tag:

*index/noindex* - Tells the search engine whether or not to index the page. By default, search engines will index a page, so the *index* parameter isn't ever needed.

*follow/nofollow* - If you have a page set to *noindex*, the *follow* parameter tells the search engine to go ahead and follow all the links on the page, passing equity as it normally would. If you set the parameter to *nofollow* then the search engine will use that as a signal not to follow or pass equity for any of the links on the page.

*noimageindex* - Tells the search engine not to index any images found on the page. However, if these images are linked from somewhere else, the engine will index them unless specifically directed not to from each source in which it is linked.

*none* - The equivalent of using both the *noindex* and *nofollow* directives.

*noarchive* - Tells the search engines not to archive the page. They can analyze it but there will be no cache available.

*nocache* - Similar to the *noarchive* but for the Internet Explorer and Firefox browsers.

*nosnippet* - Tells the search engines not to show any snippets of the page in the search results. This includes the meta description.

*unavailable_after* - Tells the search engines to stop indexing the page after a particular date.

By default, you typically can do without a *robots* meta tag. Only use it when you wish to apply any of the directives noted above.

# Meta Description Tag

*<meta name="description" content="This is your page description. Be specific and succinct so your visitors know what your page is about."/>*

A web page's meta description is intended to be a short snippet of the content provided on the page. While the title tag is extremely limited, a description allows more space to capture the essence of what the visitor will experience. By default, the meta description tag isn't seen by website visitors, but it is an important part of the search experience.

## How and Where the Meta Description is Displayed

The meta description frequently accompanies the title tag in the SERPs. The page's title is generally the clickable link, and the meta description is displayed below it. It provides the searcher with additional information about the page.

Below is an example of meta *description* tags in the search results.

www.socketmobile.com ▾

Socket Mobile: Barcode scanners for iOS and Android apps

Socket Mobile is a leading innovator of **barcode scanners** for data capture and delivery solutions for enhanced productivity.

*Screen capture from Google.com*

Google is pretty inconsistent with how it displays the description in the search results, and sometimes it does not at all. In the example above, you see the complete description content displayed in the SERPs, however depending on the search, Google may rewrite the description or pull snippets directly from the page as they have done in the example below:

www.barcodelookup.com › mobile-app ▾

Barcode Lookup Mobile App for Android and iOS Devices

Scan and save. **Barcode scanner**. Frustrated because you don't have time to compare prices at different stores? Tired ...

*Screen capture from Google.com*

The actual meta description is: *Barcode Lookup offers a free mobile app at the App Store and Google Play. Scan and retrieve barcode info including product descriptions, images and reviews.*

You can decide for yourself which one is better for a search for *barcode scanner*.

The exact formula that triggers a description snippet rewrite is anyone's guess, but if you're not happy with what Google displays, keep tweaking the description until what you want shows for your important keyword(s). Just remember what you see for one search may not be what you see for another, even for the same page showing in the SERPs.

# How You Benefit from a Strong Meta Description

A page's meta *description* doesn't factor into Google's algorithm and therefore won't help improve your search engine rankings directly. Other search engines may use them, but if they do, the weight of the tag is minimal. However, just because the meta *description* offers no ranking impact, that doesn't mean this isn't an important part of your optimization efforts.

Where the description provides its greatest value is enticing the searcher to click from the SERPs to your website. Think of it as an "assist" to the page's title tag. While the title is short and can't provide much detail, the meta *description* allows you to give more context for the page's content. Searchers use the additional information provided in the meta *description* to determine which site is most likely to meet their search needs.

As for optimization, a title tag's space limitations mean you only have room for one main keyword or topic. A description allows you to optimize for phrase variables and "long tail" phrases related to the primary topic.

Meta *description* tag length varies, though it currently sits at roughly 160 characters. But since you'll never know how much of the description will be displayed in the search results, you want to maximize the first several words. Get to the point quickly with important info toward the front and leave room for a call to action at the end.

# How to Craft a Winning Meta Description

When writing your meta *description* tags, here are a few tips to keep in mind:

**155-160 Characters Max -** Google is always fiddling with how much information displays in their search results so any rule on tag length today can be different tomorrow. What we do know is that there is no true maximum length a meta *description* can be, only a maximum length of what shows in the SERPs, which changes for each device.

**Use Keywords Early -** Since Google ignores the description for ranking purposes, any keyword usage isn't for Google, it's for the searcher. Use words that resonate with the search intent, placing them near the front. This will ensure that important words will be seen if your description is too long. Feel free to add extended qualifiers and keyword variations throughout as good sentence structure allows.

**Unique for Each Page -** Each unique page of content deserves a unique meta *description*. Meta descriptions should accurately reflect the content of each page. If the page content is different from the content of other pages, the description should differ as well.

**Be Compelling -** Above all else, your description should be compelling to the searcher. Use proper sentence structure rather than a list of keywords. The description must entice the visitor to click into your site. The more helpful it is, the more searchers will click.

## You Don't Always Need a Meta Description

Because Google tends to pull snippets from the page when warranted, you don't always need to have a meta tag. You can simply rely on Google to do the work for you. But keep in mind, in doing so, you turn the power of your messaging over to Google completely. If Google rewrites your meta tag, so be it, but at least you did what you could to provide the message you want searchers to see.

# Meta Tags Provide Important Directives

Even though meta tags are not visible on the webpage, they do provide important directives that influence what the visitor sees elsewhere. From search results to page layout, meta tags are important enough not to be ignored and are even well-deserving of your time. Ensuring your meta tags are correctly written and convey the right information is paramount to a successful website.

# HEADING TAG OPTIMIZATION

Whether you are optimizing for search rankings or visitor engagement, content headings are an important aspect of a successful optimization and user-engagement strategy. How much weight search engines give to headings is debatable, but very few SEOs believe they hold no value at all. And while they may not be the proverbial magic bullet to instantly improve your search engine rankings, optimizing heading tags for search engines and visitors is, at the very least, an important step toward a more successfully optimized web page.

## What are Heading Tags?

Heading tags are a way to segment content to be seen as page or paragraph headings. It's entirely possible to create visual headings without using any type of identifying code, however, using proper heading code ensures that search engines read your content the same way that the visitor does.

There are six heading tags you can use:

$<h1>$, $<h2>$, $<h3>$, $<h4>$, $<h5>$, and $<h6>$

The numbers represent importance, with *H1* being the highest-valued and *H6* being the least. While the *Hx* code is hidden with the rest of the HTML, the content of the tag is displayed on the page. Here is how an *H1* tag appears in HTML:

*$<h1>$This Is Often the First or Most Visible Text on the Page$</h1>$*

### Proper Heading Tag Use

The best way to illustrate how to use heading tags is to equate it to an outline of a written document or report. The *H1* would be the equivalent of the document's title.

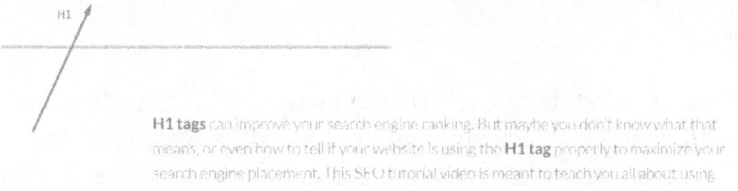

*Screen capture by Stoney deGeyter*

The *H1* doesn't necessarily have to mirror the page's title tag, but since they're both representing the content, they'll likely be pretty similar. While the title tag is limited in how much shows in the SERPs, the *H1* tag is only limited by how it appears on the page. Typically, an *H1* will be anywhere from one to a dozen words, depending on the page.

Current HTML standards allow for multiple *H1* tags per page, but only if they are in properly established containers. Typically, however, this isn't something you need. Most pages should have both a minimum and maximum of one *H1* tag. The remainder of the *Hx* tags (*H2-H6*) should be used as headings to separate content sections on the page using a traditional outline format.

Most people are familiar with how to organize a report. You have 1-3 main points (I, II, III), each followed with sub-points (A, B, and C), which also might have their own sub-points (1, 2, and 3, etc.) Since *Hx* tags are designed as level markers, not specific points, the *H2* tag would be used for each of your main points. The *H3* would be used on your sub-points and *H4* for your sub-sub points and so on.

Keep in mind that each of these points is representative of a paragraph heading. Except for pages with thousands of words, most pages don't need more than levels *H1-3*. Longer content may use all six, but that's rare. How many or what *Hx* tags you use should be determined by the needs of the content itself.

Many developers use *Hx* tags to segment content in the page template. There is nothing wrong with doing so, however, they should stick to using *H5* and *H6* tags only. This reserves *H1-4* exclusively for the main content.

There is one exception to the above. If you use sub-headlines below your main heading (similar to news articles), the *H1* would be the main headline with the sub-headline marked up as an *H2*. The rest of the content would use *H3-6* as needed.

# Benefits from Well-Structured Headings

Heading tags don't carry a lot of weight with search engines, but they do have some. Their value isn't just for search, but in how visitors experience your content. *Hx* tags add value in multiple ways:

## Consistency

Once you set the visual style of each *Hx* tag using CSS (Cascading Style Sheets), then it is easy to maintain consistency throughout your website. Simply change any piece of content to an *Hx* and the CSS takes over and makes it look the same as every other similar *Hx* tag. Without coding the *Hx* in CSS, you're relying on memory or code copy each time you use the *Hx* tags throughout your site.

## Stands Out

The font, size, and color of your headings is completely customizable. You typically want headings to stand out significantly from the standard content, with each heading number being slightly different from the previous. Starting in reverse order, the *H6* should at least be bolded (or italicized) with increases in font size as you work your way up to *H1*. The idea is for each *Hx* tag to be visually different from each other while standing out. Embellishments to make the headings stand out are good, but avoid underlining them. This will make them appear to be a link, which could be confusing to visitors.

## Improves Scanability

When properly used, headings allow readers to easily peruse and find the information that is most relevant to their particular needs. Without the ability to skim headings, readers are forced to read every word rather than being able to jump to content most relevant for their needs.

## Added Search Relevance

The search optimization impact of headings is arguable, but most SEOs agree that there is at least a minor benefit. This means you want to use your headings—especially your *H1* tag—to your greatest advantage. Inserting keywords into headings gives both search engines and visitors additional context to better understand the subject of the content directly below.

Keep keyword usage in your heading tags to a minimum, only using them when it makes logical sense to the reader. Don't try to stuff your headings with keywords as that will only produce a negative impact on both the search engine and the visitor.

# How to Craft a Strong Heading

There is no universal right or wrong way to write headings. Some are short (two to three words), while others might be five to ten word sentences. The length of the heading should be based entirely on the best way to communicate to the reader.

Each heading should represent the content that immediately follows, creating a clear trail of tease-to-fulfillment as the reader moves down the page. You generally want one heading every three or four paragraphs, though this isn't a hard and fast rule. Try to avoid using a heading for every paragraph.

When headings are used properly, reader interest and engagement will improve. Your content will have greater visibility and conversion rates due to improved accessibility for both visitors and search engines. Improving your headings may not produce a sudden jump in search engine rankings, but you may see increased conversion and engagement metrics as a result.

# DUPLICATE CONTENT ISSUES

In the arena of website architecture, there is little doubt that eliminating duplicate content can be one of the hardest fought battles. Too many content management systems and ignorant developers build sites that work great for displaying content but have little consideration for how that content functions from a search engine perspective. That often leaves damaging duplicate content dilemmas for the SEO to deal with.

In this chapter we'll explore in detail the two types of duplicate content that can impact your optimization efforts:

**On-Site Duplication** - When the same content is duplicated on two or more unique URLs of your site. Typically, this is something your site admin and web development team can control.

**Off-Site Duplication** - When two or more websites publish the same pieces of content. This is something that you often cannot control directly but requires working with third parties and the owners of any offending websites.

## Why is Duplicate Content a Problem?

The best way to explain why duplicate content is bad is to first tell you why unique content is good. Unique content is one of the best opportunities you have to set yourself apart from your competition. When the content on your site is unique, you stand out. You have something no one else has.

On the other hand, when you use the same content to describe your products or services or have content republished on other sites, you lose the advantage of being unique. Every duplicated page is just another non-unique page on the web.

Duplicate content competes against itself. Each version may attract eyeballs and links, but none will receive the full value it would get if it were the sole version. However, when valuable and unique content can be found on only one URL, that URL has the best chance of being found and ranked.

Look at the illustration below. If the letter A represents content that is duplicated on two URLs, and B through Q represents pages linking to that content, the value passed from pages B through Q is split between both URLs.

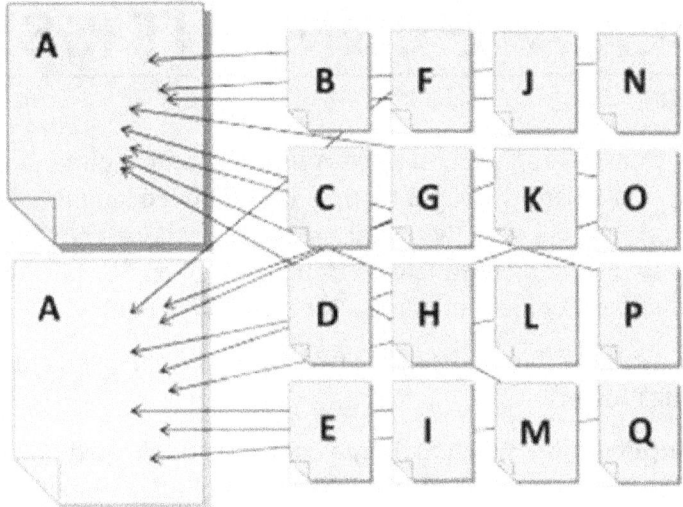

*Illustration by Stoney deGeyter*

Now imagine if pages B-Q all linked to only one page A. Instead of splitting the value each link provides, all the value would go to a single URL instead, which increases the chances of that content ranking in search.

# Off-Site Duplicate Content

As stated above, off-site duplication is generally something for which you have little or no control. There are three primary sources for this type of duplication:

1. Third-party content you have republished on your website. For ecommerce sites, this is often in the form of generic product descriptions provided by the manufacturer.
2. Your content that has been republished on third-party sites with your approval. This is usually in the form of article distribution or descriptions of your own products that other sellers post on their sites.
3. Content that someone has stolen from your site and republished without your approval.
4. Content that belongs to your company, but which is duplicated on multiple domains (often due to making content availble in multiple languages or for multiple countries).

Let's look at each.

## Content Scrapers and Thieves

Content scrapers are one of the biggest offenders in creating off-site duplicate content. Spammers and other nefarious perpetrators build tools that grab content from other websites and republish it. For the most part, these scrapers use your content to generate traffic to their sites to get visitors to click on ads. (Yeah, I'm looking at you, Google.)

Unfortunately, there isn't much you can do about these perpetrators other than to submit a copyright infringement report to Google in hopes that it will be removed from the search index. In many cases, submitting these reports can be a full-time job.

Of course, you have the option to ignore it completely, hoping Google can tell the difference between a quality site (yours) and the site(s) your scraped content is on. This is hit and miss as I've sometimes seen scraped content rank higher than the originating source.

One semi-effective hack against these thieves and scrapers is to use absolute URLs when you are linking to your internal pages. Any links pointing to other pages of your site are often taken as-is. Any scraped content will provide a link back to your site.

You can also try adding a canonical tag back to the source page (a good practice regardless). If the scrapers grab any of this code, the canonical tag will at least provide a signal for Google to recognize you as the originator.

However these strategies rely on scrapers taking content exactly as is, and many of them are advanced enough now to replace any instances to your domain with their own.

## Article Distribution

Several years ago, it seemed like every SEO was republishing their content on "ezines" as a link building tactic. When Google cracked down on content quality and link schemes, republishing fell by the wayside. But with the right focus, it can be a solid marketing strategy. Notice that I said *marketing*, not *SEO* strategy.

For the most part, any time you're publishing content on other websites, they want the unique rights to that content. Why? Because they don't want multiple versions of that content on the web devaluing what the publisher has to offer. But as Google has gotten better about assigning rights to the content originator (better, but not perfect), many publishers now allow content to be reused on the author's personal sites as well.

Does this create a duplicate content problem? In a small way, it does. With two versions of the content available, each can be generating links. This can create a bit of competition between them. But in the end, if the number of duplicate versions is limited and controlled, the impact will be limited as well. In fact, the primary downside lands on the author rather than the secondary publisher. The first published version of the content will generally be credited as the canonical version. In all but a few cases, these publishers will get more value from the content than the author's website that republishes it.

All this being said, it's often a good idea to republish content that you write on your own website, because publishers update their websites, remove older or outdated articles, or close up entirely. It is a good idea to keep a copy of your content so that it's always available for you to refer back to.

## Generic Product Descriptions

Some of the most common forms of duplicated content comes from product descriptions that are reused by each (and almost every) seller. A lot of online retailers sell the same products as thousands of other stores. In most cases, the product descriptions are provided by the manufacturer, which is then uploaded into each site's database and presented on their product pages. While the layout of the pages will be different, the bulk of the product page content (product descriptions) will be identical.

Now multiply that across millions of different products and hundreds of thousands of websites selling those products, and you can wind up with a lot of content that is, to put it mildly, not unique. How does a search engine differentiate between one or another when a search is performed? On a purely content-analysis level, it can't. This means the search engine must look at other signals to decide which one should rank.

One of these signals is links. Get more links and you can win the bland content sweepstakes. But if you're up against a more powerful competitor, you may have a long battle to fight before you can catch them in the link building department. Which brings you back to looking for another competitive advantage.

The best way to achieve that is by taking the extra effort to write unique descriptions for each product. Depending on the number of products you offer, this could end up being quite the challenge, but in the end, it'll be well worth it. Take a look at the illustration below. If all the gray pages represent the same product with the same product descriptions, the yellow represents the same product with a unique description. If you were Google, which one would you want to rank higher?

*Illustration by Stoney deGeyter*

Pages with unique content will have an inherent advantage over duplicate content. That may or may not be enough to outrank your competitors, but it surely is the baseline to stand out, not just to Google, but to your customers as well.

# On-Site Duplicate Content

Technically, Google treats all duplicate content the same. In practical terms, that makes on-site duplicate content no different than off-site. But on-site duplication is less forgivable because, unlike off-site, you have far more control over this type of duplication. And as far as your SEO efforts go, when you have on-site duplication, you're shooting yourself in the proverbial foot.

On-site content duplication often stems from bad site architecture. When developers or content management solutions don't follow search-friendly best practices, you lose the ability to give your content the best opportunity to rank well in search results.

Some argue against the need for good architecture, citing Google propaganda about how search engines can "figure it out." The problem with this is that it relies entirely on Google actually figuring it out. Yes, Google can determine that some duplicate content should be considered the same, and the algorithms may take this into account when analyzing your site, but that's no guarantee they will. Another way to look at it is that just because you know someone smart doesn't mean they'll be able to protect you from your own stupidity! If you leave things to Google and Google fails, you're in trouble.

## Product Categorization Duplication

Far too many ecommerce sites create duplication with their product categorization options. As we'll go over in the Product Category Pages chapter, this duplication is caused by content management systems that create unique product URLs for every category a product is tagged in. This in itself isn't bad (and can be great for the visitor), but by doing this, the CMS generates multiple URLs for each product.

If you're on a home repair site looking for a book on installing bathroom flooring,you might find the book you're looking for by following any of these navigation paths:

- Home > flooring > bathroom > books
- Home > bathroom > books > flooring
- Home > books > flooring > bathroom

Each of these is a viable navigation path, but the problem arises when a unique URL

is generated for each path:

- *https://www.myfakesite.com/flooring/bathroom/books/fake-book-by-fake-author*
- *https://www.myfakesite.com/bathroom/books/flooring/fake-book-by-fake-author*
- *https://www.myfakesite.com/books/flooring/bathroom/fake-book-by-fake-author*

I've seen sites like this create up to ten URLs for every product. This turns a 5k product website into a site with 45 thousand duplicate pages! That is a problem. If our example URLs above generated a total of ten links, those links would end up being split three ways. Whereas, if a competitor's page for the same product got the same ten links to only a single URL, that URL has a far greater chance of ranking. Instead of 3-4 links for a page, they get the value of all ten.

Not only that, but search engines also limit their crawl bandwidth so they can spend it on indexing unique and valuable content. When your site has that many duplicate pages, there is a strong chance the engine will stop crawling before it even gets a fraction of your unique content indexed. This means hundreds of valuable pages won't be available in search results and those that are indexed are duplicates competing against each other.

## The (Best) Solution

One fix to this problem is to only tag products for a single category rather than multiples. That solves the duplication issue, but it's not necessarily the best solution for the shoppers since it eliminates the other navigation paths to find products they want.

So, scratch that one off the list.

If you don't have the option of assigning a master category (more on that below), the best solution is to remove any type of categorization from the URLs altogether. This way, no matter the navigation path used to find the product, the product URL itself is always the same, and might look something like this:

- *https://www.myfakesite.com/products/fake-book-by-fake-author*

This fixes the duplication without changing how the visitor navigates to the products. The downside to this method is that you lose the category keywords in the URL. Category names may provide only a small benefit to the totality of SEO, but every little bit helps.

If you want to take your solution to the next level; to get the most optimization value possible while keeping the user experience, build an option that allows each product to be assigned to a "master" category in addition to others. When a master category is in play, the product can be found through the multiple navigation paths, but the product page uses no more than a single URL.

That might make your product URL look something like this:

- *https://www.myfakesite.com/flooring/fake-book-by-fake-author* OR
- *https://www.myfakesite.com/bathroom/fake-book-by-fake-author* OR
- *https://www.myfakesite.com/books/fake-book-by-fake-author*

This latter solution is the best overall, though it does take some additional programming. However, there are a couple of other relatively easy "solutions" to implement, but I only consider them a band-aid until a better solution can be implemented.

## Alternative Solution #1

Because the master-categorization option isn't always available with out of the box CMS or ecommerce solutions, there is an alternative option that will "help" solve the duplicate content problem. This involves adding a *noindex* robots meta tag. This tag tells search engines not to index the URLs that you don't want.

Unfortunately, this solution isn't always viable, as the CMS will often add the *noindex* tag to all the URLs a product uses, including the one you want to keep. There are clever workarounds, but you'll have to weigh the benefits of implementing them against the value gained.

## Alternative Solution #2

The better band-aid solution for this issue is to implement canonical tags on all product pages. Some CMS platforms already do this for you.

The canonical tag simply tells the search engines which URL is your preference.

*<link rel="canonical" href="https://www.myfakesite.com/books/fake-book-by-fake-author" />*

Theoretically, this tells the search engines not to index any non-canonical URLs it finds and assign all value metrics over to the canonical URL. This works most of the time, but in reality, the search engines only use the canonical tag as a "signal," rather than a directive. They'll apply or ignore it as they see fit. However, since the content on all the additional URLs should be an almost exact duplicate (except any breadcrumb trails on the page) the search engines should honor it.

## Redundant URL Duplication

For the benefit of those jumping around and reading chapters out of order, I'm going to create my own a bit of duplicate content covering similar ground as in a previous chapter. (Oh, the irony!)

One of the most basic website architectural issues revolves around how pages are accessed in the browser. By default, almost every page of your site can be accessed using a slightly different URL. If left unchecked, each URL leads to the same page with the same content.

Considering the home page alone, it can likely be accessed using four different URLs:

- *http://site.com*
- *http://www.site.com*
- *https://site.com*
- *https://www.site.com*

And when dealing with internal pages, you can get an additional version of each URL by adding a trailing slash:

- *http://site.com/page*
- *http://site.com/page/*

- *http://www.site.com/page*

- *http://www.site.com/page/*

That's up to eight alternate URLs for each page! Of course, Google should know that all these URLs should be treated as one, but which one?

## The Solution

Aside from the canonical tag, which we addressed already, the solution here is to ensure all alternate versions of the URLs redirect to the canonical URL. Keep in mind, this isn't just a home page issue. The same issue applies to every one of your site URLs. Therefore, the redirects implemented should be global.

If possible, set each redirect to the canonical version. For instance, if the canonical URL is *https://www.site.com*, each redirect should point there rather than going through multiple hops like this:

- *Site.com > https://site.com > https://www.site.com*

- *Site.com > www.site.com > https://www.site.com*

Instead, the redirects should look like this:

- *http://site.com > https://www.site.com/*

- *http://www.site.com > https://www.site.com/*

- *https://site.com > https://www.site.com/*

- *https://www.site.com > https://www.site.com/*

- *http://site.com/ > https://www.site.com/*

- *http://www.site.com/ > https://www.site.com/*

- *https://site.com/ > https://www.site.com/*

By reducing the number of redirect hops, you speed up page load, reduce server bandwidth, and have less that can go wrong along the way.

Finally, you'll need to make sure all internal links in the site point to the canonical version as well. While the redirect should solve the duplicate problem, redirects can fail if something goes wrong on the server. If that happens, even temporarily, having only the canonical pages linked internally can help prevent a sudden surge of duplicate content issues from popping up.

## URL Parameters and Query Strings

Years ago, the usage of session IDs created a major duplicate content problem for SEOs. Today's technology, however, has made session IDs all but obsolete, but another problem has arisen that is just as bad, if not worse: URL parameters.

Parameters are used to pull fresh content from the server, usually based on one or more filters or selections being made. The two examples below show alternate URLs for a single page: *site.com/shirts/*. The first shows the shirts filtered by *color*, *size*, and *style*, the second URL shows shirts sorted by *price*, then to display a certain number of products to show per page,

- *Site.com/shirts/?color=red&size=small&style=long_sleeve*
- *Site.com/shirts/?sort=price&display=12*

Based on these filters alone, there are three viable URLs that the search engines can find. But the order of these parameters can change based on the order in which they were chosen, which means you might get several more accessible URLs like this:

- *Site.com/shirts/?size=small&color=red&style=long_sleeve*
- *Site.com/shirts/?size=small&style=long_sleeve&color=red*
- *Site.com/shirts/?display=12&sort=price*

And this

- *Site.com/shirts/?size=small&color=red&style=long_sleeve&display=12&sort=price*
- *Site.com/shirts/?display=12&size=small&color=red&sort=price*
- *Site.com/shirts/?size=small&display=12&sort=price&color=red&style=long_sleeve*

Most of these additional URLs won't produce unique content. Of the parameters above, the only one you might want to have as a standalone landing page is *style*. The rest, not so much.

### The Solution

Strategically planning your navigation and URL structure is critical for getting out ahead of duplicate content problems. Part of that process includes understanding the difference between having a legitimate landing page and a page that allows visitors to filter results.

Landing page (and canonical) URLs should look like this:

- *Site.com/shirts/long-sleeve/*
- *Site.com/shirts/v-neck/*
- *Site.com/shirts/collared/*

And the filtered results URLs would look something like this:

- *Site.com/shirts/long-sleeve/?size=small&color=red&display=12&sort=price*
- *Site.com/shirts/v-neck/?color=red*
- *Site.com/shirts/collared/?size=small&display=12&sort=price&color=red*

With properly established URLs, you can do two things: 1) Add the correct canonical tag to the code (everything before the *?* in the URL), and 2) go into Google Search Console and tell Google to ignore all the other parameters.

If you consistently use parameters only for filtering and sorting content, you won't have to worry about accidentally telling Google not to crawl a valuable parameter… because none of them are. But because the canonical tag is only a signal, you must complete step two to achieve the best results. And remember this only affects Google. You have to do the same with Bing.

## Pro Developer Tip

Search engines typically ignore everything to the right of the # symbol in the URL. If you program that into every URL before the parameter, you won't have to worry about the canonical being only a band-aid solution:

- *Site.com/shirts/long-sleeve/#?size=small&color=red&display=12&sort=price*
- *Site.com/shirts/v-neck/#?color=red*
- *Site.com/shirts/collared/#?size=small&display=12&sort=price&color=red*

If search engines were to access the URLs above, they would only index the canonical part of the URL and ignore the rest. Though search engines can choose to change this at any time.

## Ad Landing Page and A/B Test Duplication

It's not uncommon for marketers to create numerous versions of similar content, either as landing pages for ads or for A/B/multivariate testing purposes. This will often give you some great data and feedback, but if those pages are open for search engines to spider and index, it can cause duplicate content problems.

## The Solution

Rather than using a canonical tag to point back to the master page, as has been suggested previously, this type of duplication requires another solution altogether.

Pages of this type tend to be orphans, without any direct links to them from inside the site. This won't prevent search engines from finding them, however. The canonical tag is designed to transfer page value and authority to the primary page, but since you don't want these pages to be accessible beyond their intended purpose, the best solution is to keep them out of the index.

To do that, you can tell Google not to crawl the page via the robots.txt file, but that won't keep it from appearing in the search results. That leaves the robots meta tag with a *noindex* directive as the best solution.

*<meta name="robots" content="noindex">*

Google will still crawl the page (if it finds it) but this directive prevents them from including it in the search results. Now, the only way for it to be accessed is through a direct link, and that is mostly controllable.

# When Duplicate Content Isn't (Much of) a Problem

One of the most common SEO myths is that there is a duplicate content penalty. There isn't. At least no more than there is a penalty for not putting gas in your car and letting it run empty. Google does not actively penalize duplicate content, but that doesn't mean there are not natural consequences that occur because of it.

Without the threat of penalty, marketers have a little more flexibility in deciding which consequences they are willing to live with. While I would argue that you should aggressively eliminate on-site duplicate content entirely, offsite duplication may actually create more value than consequences.

Getting valuable content republished off-site can help you build brand recognition in a way that publishing it on your own can't. That's because many off-site publishers have a bigger audience and a vastly larger social reach. Publishing your content on your website may reach thousands of eyeballs, but published off-site, it might reach hundreds of thousands.

Many publishers expect to maintain exclusive rights to the content they publish, but some allow you to repurpose it on your own site after a short waiting period. This allows you to get the additional exposure the other platform provides but still have the opportunity to build your audience on your site.

To be effective, this type of article distribution must be limited. If you shoot your content out to hundreds of other sites to be republished, the value of that content diminishes exponentially. And typically, it does little to reinforce your brand because the sites willing to publish mass duplicated content are of little value to begin with.

Weigh the pros and cons carefully. If duplication with a lot of branding outweighs the smaller authority value you'd get with unique content on your own site, then, by all means, pursue a measured republishing strategy. But the keyword there is *measured*. You don't want to republish *all* your informational content, otherwise you'll undercut the value you're trying to create for your brand.

By understanding the problems, solutions, and in some cases, value of duplicate content, you can begin the process of eliminating the duplication you don't want and pursuing the duplication you do. Ultimately, your goal is to build a site that is known for strong, unique content, and use that content to get the highest value possible.

# CONVERSION OPTIMIZATION

One of the primary goals of digital marketing is to drive targeted traffic to your website. Search engines are still a significant driver of traffic, but social media, word of mouth, and online advertising are also effective means to generate visits. However, traffic is just one aspect of a successful marketing campaign. What happens after a visitor arrives is of vital importance as well.

Driving even the most highly-targeted traffic to your site doesn't guarantee you'll convert a single visitor into a customer. But let's take a step back. Conversion optimization typically focuses on the visitors that land on your website, but *effective* conversion optimization starts long before that. Let's look at how you can "prime the pump" to increase the probability of turning your site traffic into paying customers.

## Keywords that Convert

There are two kinds of targeted visitors: Those who are ready to buy and those who are not *yet* ready to buy. The trick is knowing which keywords drive which kind of traffic.

Choose any keyword phrase and by simply making a couple of tweaks, it can drive one type of visitor or the other. While all targeted traffic can be turned into a customer, you'll have a far greater chance of converting a visitor who's closer to buying now than one who isn't. Getting people to your site before they are ready to buy is a branding opportunity. We all know when someone leaves without making a purchase though, the odds of them returning to do so are greatly diminished. I'm not saying don't focus on this traffic, but in terms of priority, spend the bulk of your optimization time focused on those who can be converted now rather than later.

It's true, keywords that drive this ready-to-buy traffic have much lower search volume numbers, but that's because there are so many nuanced variables in keyword usage. Add those nuances together and you will find the opportunity is equal to if not greater than the smaller pool of higher-traffic keywords.

The keywords you focus on make a huge difference in your conversion rate. A searcher looking for a *motorcycle* isn't necessarily ready to buy a motorcycle. They may be researching what kind of motorcycle they want to buy, but they just don't know yet. However, someone searching for a *2015 honda gold wing* is a lot closer to knowing what kind of motorcycle they want. For them, it's a matter of working out the details and finding the right place to buy. Even though there are substantially more searchers typing in the single-word term, more sales will likely be generated from the far less frequently searched four-word phase.

Continuing with this example, once you factor in all the years, makes, and models of all the motorcycles you might sell, you're looking at significant numbers of ready-to-buy searchers making their way to your site.

Far too often, marketers focus on the high-volume keywords simply because more traffic looks great in analytics reports. And yes, those keywords do generate sales, as visitors are moved from the *research* to the *ready-to-buy* phase, but conversion rates will be far less substantial than on the high-converting keywords. And those *research* keywords take a lot more time and effort to rank.

By focusing on the more highly targeted *buy* phrases—at least initially—you may drive less traffic, but the result will often produce a better conversion rate..

# Compelling Titles & Descriptions

Focusing on the right keywords allows you to achieve top rankings for your ready-to-convert audience. Getting those searchers to click into your site is another matter altogether. With all the competition and clutter on that first page of results, enticing the click to your website is no easy task.

In the race to get clicks from the search results, you have three tools at your disposal:

- The ranking itself: the higher you appear in the SERPs; the more traffic you are likely to get.
- The title tag that search engines typically use as the clickable link to your site.
- The meta description that search engines typically display below the title.

In previous chapters, we detailed how to successfully optimize your tags. Suffice it to say, a page's title and meta description are significant factors in bringing targeted traffic to each page. And as discussed previously, it's not all about rankings. A compelling title and description can often drive more traffic from a lower-ranking position than the sites ranked above it.

Be sure the optimization of your title and meta description tags goes beyond keywords. Think about how best you can compel the visitor to click on *your* listing rather than a competitor's.

# Understand the Visitor's Need

Assuming searchers click on your result and land on your page, you still have a way to go before you can turn that click into a conversion. The rest of this chapter will focus on the visitor's overall experience on the website and how to make sure the site itself meets is exactly what they are looking for.

Earlier we talked about searchers being in different mindsets. Going back to a previous example, a search for *motorcycle* requires vastly different content than a search for *2015 honda gold wing*. The first searcher is looking for high-level information. They are in the early research phases. The second searcher has likely performed a good deal of research and is in the final stages. They are inching closer to being ready to commit to the purchase if they are not there already.

| "motorcycle" | "2015 honda gold wing" |
|---|---|
| • Research phase<br>• Needs high level info<br>• Send to a product/service category page | • Ready-to-buy phase<br>• Needs specific information<br>• Send to specific product page matching search query |

*Illustration by Stoney deGeyter*

While both of these searchers are looking for a motorcycle, you can't drop both searchers onto the same page. If you deliver the *gold wing* searcher onto a generic page about motorcycles, they are highly likely to hit the back button rather than look around the page to find the Hondas and then the Goldwings.

Similarly, if you deliver the *motorcycle* searcher to a page exclusively about Honda Gold Wing motorcycles, you've given them content they are not ready for. In both cases, the content isn't a good match for what the searchers want.

If you fail to deliver the right content, you will often send searchers looking elsewhere, and drastically reduce the likelihood of them becoming a customer.

# Value and Trust

Trust is a significant factor in the sales process. If your site fails at communicating your trustworthiness, your visitors will be inclined to make their purchase elsewhere. When looking at two otherwise equal websites, the site that's able to inspire the greatest confidence wins.

There are many ways in which you can convey trust. It's known that visitors make a snap judgment about your site within a second of landing on it. This judgment may even be subconscious. What does the look and feel of your website convey to your visitor?

The content plays an important role. Aside from matching intent, as discussed above, does your content provide the information the visitor is seeking? If you can't provide the information that they want, how do you expect to convince the visitor that you'll deliver the product or service they need? Your content must be effective at providing the needed information and doing so in a way that instills trust that you're the company to do business with.

But it's not just the entrance page content that matters to visitors. It's the content throughout your site. A well-structured *About Us* page, comprehensive privacy and security policies, a visible phone number or other contact info, security assurances, organizations you belong to, etc., are all valuable tools to build visitor trust.

A recognizable brand name can help as well. You may never be as recognizable as Pepsi or Nike, but you can use social media to build up your brand recognition. People tend to buy from sites they're familiar with, even if that familiarity is superficial. The familiarity may be as superficial as seeing your social media posts. The Nikes and Pepsis of the world spend millions on branding. They know that it helps them maintain not only their market share but also their dominant authority.

Another way to build trust is through word of mouth. Let your customers be your brand ambassadors. One way to do that is to post testimonials throughout your site—not just on a testimonials page. Give visitors a chance to see what others say about you as they peruse your site.

The screenshot below shows how you might incorporate a testimonial onto your pages.

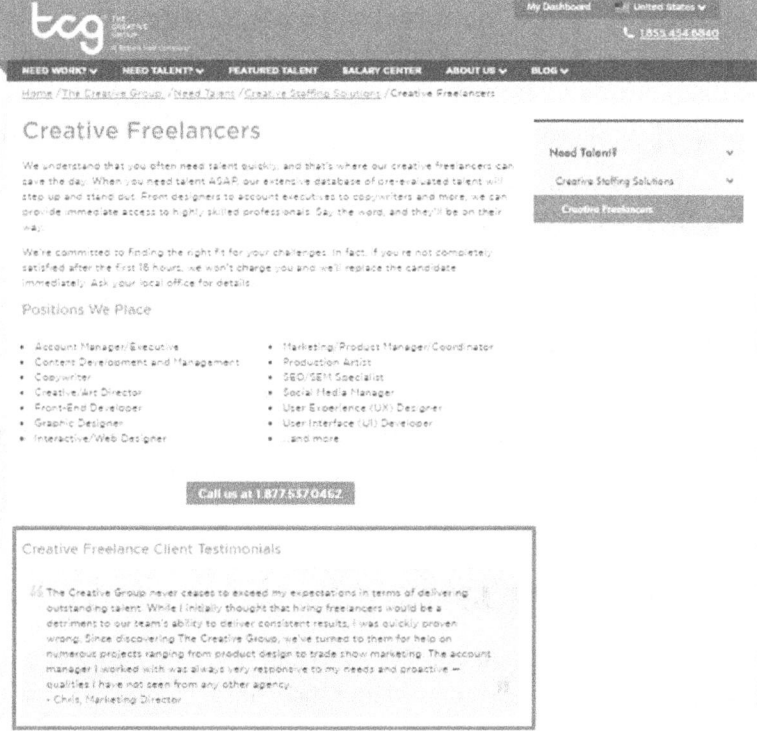

*Screen capture by Stoney deGeyter*

Reviews make great content that you don't have to write yourself, and they add to the comfort and security visitors need before becoming a customer. Be careful not to post only glowing reviews. If all your reviews are perfect, visitors will wonder if they're authentic. That said, if you're providing quality products and services, the reviews will naturally skew positive.

# Conversion Process

Every site needs to have a process to move visitors from the entry page to a conversion point. In fact, there should be many conversion processes throughout the site.

A website is like a choose-your-own-adventure novel. A visitor lands on any one of dozens or hundreds of pages and has multiple options to get themselves to the goal. One might go right for the conversion, another might detour to the About Us page, yet another might dig into warranty and shipping information, and still another might bookmark the page to return later for more research.

And while the options the visitor has may be vast, your job is to provide the single best route (or routes) to the conversion. Every page of your website should have at least one action for the visitor to take. That might be to view one or more products, "buy now", or even to subscribe to a newsletter. Whatever the primary action you want visitors to take is, make sure it's clear and obvious.

But since not every visitor is ready for that action, it's a good idea to offer a secondary call to action as well. These might be actions that lead the visitor down the trail of trust before they commit to the purchase.

Once your primary call to action is established, everything on the page should support driving the visitor to take that action. The content, the images, and the buttons or links used are important. The secondary actions are provided as a safety net if the visitor isn't ready to pull the trigger on the primary action.

Not all actions lead to the big conversion. Let visitors choose from multiple options to keep them engaged with your content until they are ready to become a customer.

## Not All Traffic is Equal

The process to turn traffic into customers starts before the visitor even arrives on your website and continues until they have completed the sale.

Always look for ways to improve your visitors' on-site experience both before and after they get to your site. By focusing on your customer's experience, you will greatly increase your conversions without ever having to increase the number of visitors.

# PRODUCT CATEGORY PAGE OPTIMIZATION

Optimizing your products involves two key page types:

- Product category pages
- Product detail pages

Each of these pages plays a critical role in driving traffic and converting those visitors into customers. While this section is all about products, the same principles can be applied for a service-based business.

Except for searchers who land directly onto a product detail page, most visitors will arrive at those pages by navigating through a product category page first. We'll address the product detail pages in the next chapter, keeping this one focused on the category pages visitors pass through on the way to the products.

Every product category page should have a specific focus. The goal is to display products that fit the category (regardless of how specific or broad) and provide the information needed to entice visitors to click to a specific product page.

Within that framework, there are some very specific optimization strategies that you need to employ to ensure each product category page is effective.

## Proper Category Page Categorization

Building effective product category pages starts with creating an effective categorization structure for your products. This means strategically constructing your product categories and sub-categories to help visitors narrow down their choices to find the product(s) that best fit their interests and needs.

### The Wrong Way to Categorize Your Products

Before we look at how to properly categorize, let's explore a poorly implemented solution. Sometimes knowing what not to do can help us better understand the right way to do it.

The example below was pulled from an apartment rental website's main navigation.

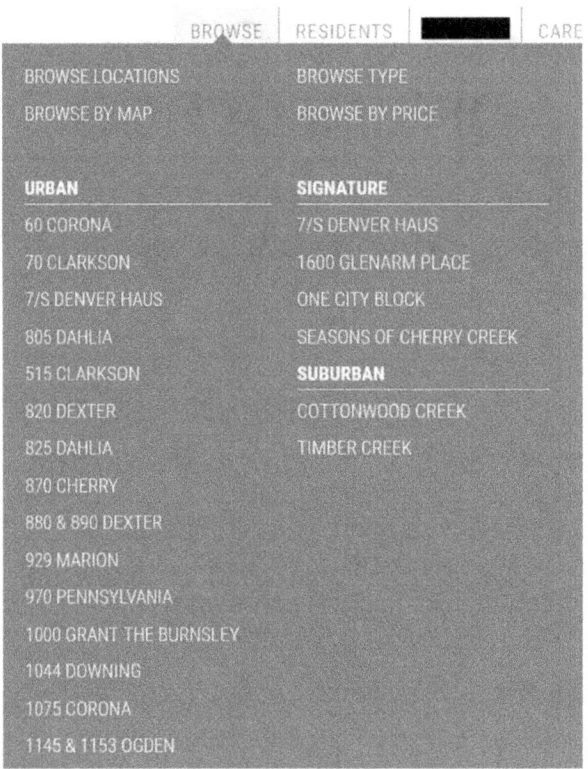

*Screen capture by Stoney deGeyter*

Notice the category headings: *Urban, Signature, Suburban.* Two of these assume people are choosing apartments based on whether they want to be in an urban or suburban environment. A little keyword research tells us that this isn't a top priority of apartment hunters. The third option, *Signature,* has no meaning, especially in relation to the other two categories.

Beyond those categories, the product page links (the actual apartment locations) aren't all that helpful unless visitors know the exact address where they want to live. Searchers unfamiliar with these addresses would have to click on each address just to know whether the location has the features and amenities they want.

This navigation is built solely for apartment hunters that are already familiar with each location and consider amenities secondary to location. Again, research shows that as a general rule, this isn't the case. This means categorizing the navigation this way effectively cuts out a large portion of the audience they want as renters.

The navigation menu offers a few more filtering options at the top that are slightly more helpful, but not much, as they cater to the same audience. Only *browse by price* and *browse by map* provide value to the average apartment hunter.

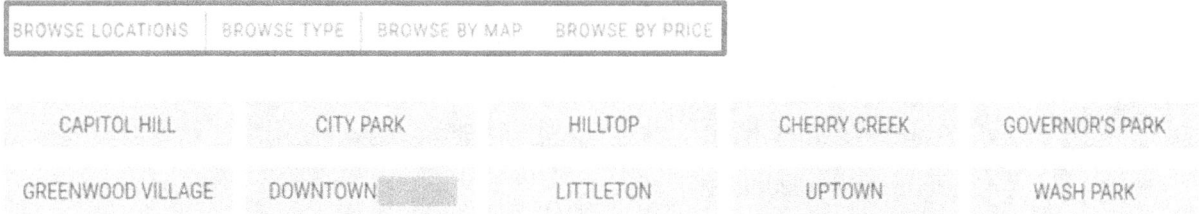

*Screen capture by Stoney deGeyter*

All told, the categorization offered in the navigation offers little to help visitors find an apartment based on the criteria that are important to them, such as the number of bedrooms or available amenities. That's not to say that neighborhood and style are not important, but those are usually secondary factors. This navigation focuses on wants as opposed to needs, which is exactly backward from the way research shows people hunt for apartments.

## The Right Way to Categorize Your Products

Let's look at what you should do to build proper product categorization. If you start with keyword research, you'll learn a lot about how people search for apartments and what types of things they are looking for. With this information, you can create product categories and sub-categories. This will, in turn, allow you to create optimized landing pages that will cover 90% of what apartment searchers are looking for.

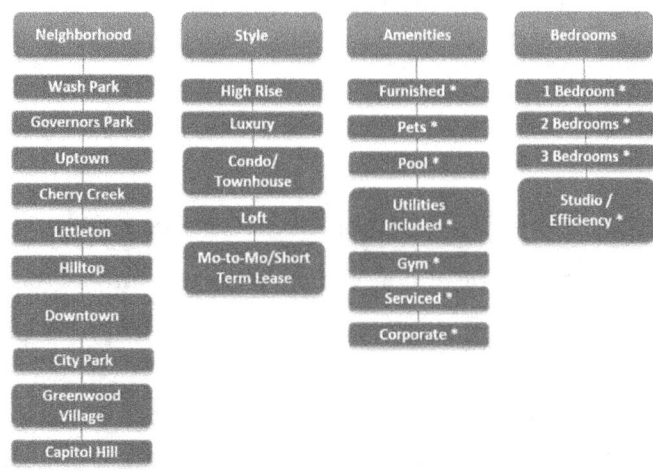

*Illustration by Stoney deGeyter*

*Note: The astrics in the image above were used to indicate to the client that these pages could also be used as filter tags.*

This navigation captures searchers who are searching one of four ways:

- General location (neighborhood)
- Type of apartment (style)
- Amenities they want
- Bedrooms needed

Those, of course, are just the broad categories. Each category can have its own set of sub-categories to capture seekers who have an even more clear idea of what they are want and need.

Just going by the categories above, each of those can be an effective landing page that will help drive searchers to a list of available apartments that most closely match their search need. From there, searchers should be able to further filter the results until they get only the available apartments that fit all their criteria.

For example, let's say someone is looking for a furnished apartment. That's their most important criteria, so they start their search there. They land on the furnished apartment page under Amenities and are immediately treated to all available furnished apartments. From here, they use real-time filtering to locate a 2-bedroom furnished condo that has a gym in the Hilltop area. Or they find a furnished 1-bedroom loft in uptown. By using these categorizations as a starting point, apartment seekers can land on the page that meets their number one need, and then filter down to see which ones that fit their need also fit their wants.

Every searcher is different, but this categorization provides the top-level needs for almost all searchers. Your goal is to build something similar. Use keyword research to create a navigation structure that allows visitors to find your products based on how they think, not how you categorize them.

## Quick Quiz

Which of the following provides better product classifications?

- Top-level categories for motorcycle helmets and motorcycle gloves, or
- Top-level categories for Men's Gear, Women's Gear, and Children's Gear.

Most people would think the second but it's the first. Even if a strong number of searchers are looking for *gear*, the only thing this categorization shows them is you have gear for men, women, and children. It doesn't indicate what kind of gear you offer.

By focusing on the actual products being sold, you can offer pages that filter for men, women, and children within each category while making sure your actual products are what the visitor sees when they land on the site. *Gear* is vague and forces the visitor to pick who they are shopping for before they get to pick what they want to buy. And for all you know, they are shopping for a man, a woman, *and* children. Focus on the product type first, then segment by audience type.

## Quick Tips

When determining your site's product categorization structure, get out somesticky notes and a nice wall or table to stick them on. After performing keyword research, write each possible product category on an individual sticky note. Create as many options as you found in your research, and then organize your categories into primary groups and sub-groups. Some categories will be redundant and others will be deemed non-essential, but it's better to start with a complete list and toss some out than not have the right categories to begin with.

By the time you're done, you should have a small handful of main product categories and dozens of sub-categories. Keep organizing until you're satisfied with the result.

One final tip: Your top-tier product categories should be your website's main navigation options. Don't hide these under a navigation option for *Products*, *Services*, or worse, *Browse*. Let visitors see what you offer upon first glance.

# Category Pages are Landing Pages

You want to think of every product category as a possible landing page. With proper optimization, visitors can land directly on these pages from the search results after performing category-level searches. I mention this above, but if you go back and look at the navigation layout I created, you can see easily how each of them can be a great entry point for top-level searchers.

To properly optimize these category/landing pages, you need to know the purpose of each page. Be sure to provide the content that serves that purpose and helps the visitor move on to the products that best fit their needs.

## Customized Heading Tag

A heading tag on a product category page does not need to do more than accurately reflect the category. Ideally, you want the visitor to do a quick skim to confirm they are landing on the right page. If you can slip in an additional value word or two, go for it, but don't add so much that the visitor has to think twice about where they are.

In the example below, the heading reads "Apartments in Capitol Hill." This is perfectly fine as it is; however, there's nothing wrong with adding the word "Affordable" to it if it is both accurate and something that will resonate with the reader.

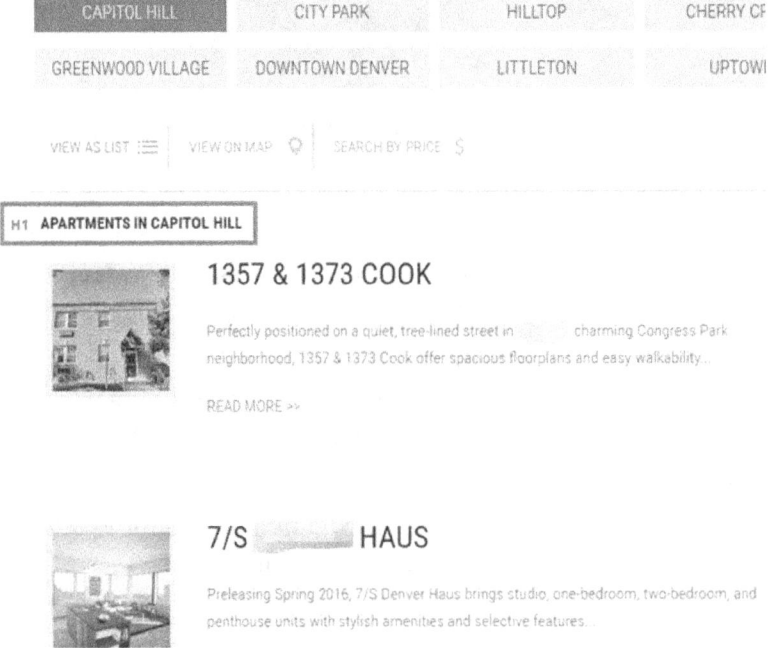

*Screen capture by Stoney deGeyter*

If you want to add even more enticement and value to your heading, consider placing a sub-headline below your main heading. Newspapers, books, and magazines use this format a lot. Stick to the facts in the main heading and follow that with the value-added statement.

Just make sure that your topmost heading on the page is wrapped in an *H1* tag. The sub-heading, if you choose to use it, should be an *H2*.

## Optimized Content

There's a difference between what visitors want and what they need. What they need is often what helps them get what they want, but this isn't always something they recognize. A great example of this is Google's "I'm Feeling Lucky" button. In 2007, Google estimated that only 1% of searchers use that button and keeping the button costs Google $110M per year in lost revenue by bypassing ads. But Google keeps the button.

Why?

Google determined that removing the button would create an even greater cost in the loss of brand perception. Searchers don't really want the "I'm feeling lucky" button, but they need to see it for Google to maintain their perception of being a "fun" company.

Content on your product category pages serves much the same purpose. Shoppers just want to buy a product, so it makes sense to dispense with unnecessary content that "gets in the way" of the shopping experience. Yet, content on these pages can provide much-needed assurances and value statements about your products that will improve your ability to capture the sale. So even if you (or your visitors) think that content is unneeded, removing it can harm more than help. And that's not even considering the search optimization value of having it.

Content is a mechanism to provide visitors valuable information about the products they wish to explore. Some will read it, some won't. Those who don't need it don't care that it's there, provided it doesn't impede their shopping experience. Those that do need it will be less likely to buy without it.

## Searcher Intent

Another key component of optimizing your product category pages is to make sure everything on the page is designed to meet the searcher's intent. For example, if a searcher is looking for *honda motorcycle batteries,* you want them to land on a page specific to Honda batteries, and not a page for all batteries. Similarly, if they are looking for *women's ski boots* don't land them on a page that includes ski boots for men and children.

Keep visitors from having to do more than a minimal amount of work once they land on your site. If they want to filter further, great, but don't make them filter products on your site just to get to what they searched for to begin with. Be sure you focus the content of the page on meeting the searcher's needs.

# On-Demand Content

One of the primary hurdles tooptimize product category pages is to find a way to integrate content while maintaining the aesthetics and usability of the page. Any text added at the top tends to push the products below the fold, forcing the shopper to scroll to see it. This can make the page appear to be a content page rather than the product category page that it is.

One solution is to place the content at the bottom of the page where it won't "interfere" with the sales process. The problem with this is that it doesn't help the sales process either. Both visitors and search engines will largely ignore the content based on its placement on the page.

Fortunately, most product category pages don't need more than a single paragraph of content to provide the needed, relevant information about the products listed. A good designer can work in four lines of content above the products without negatively impacting the page's ability to meet the customer's needs.

But what if you need more content for the sake of sales and messaging?

The answer to that is to make all but the first paragraph hidden by default, but available on demand. Here is a site that did just that:

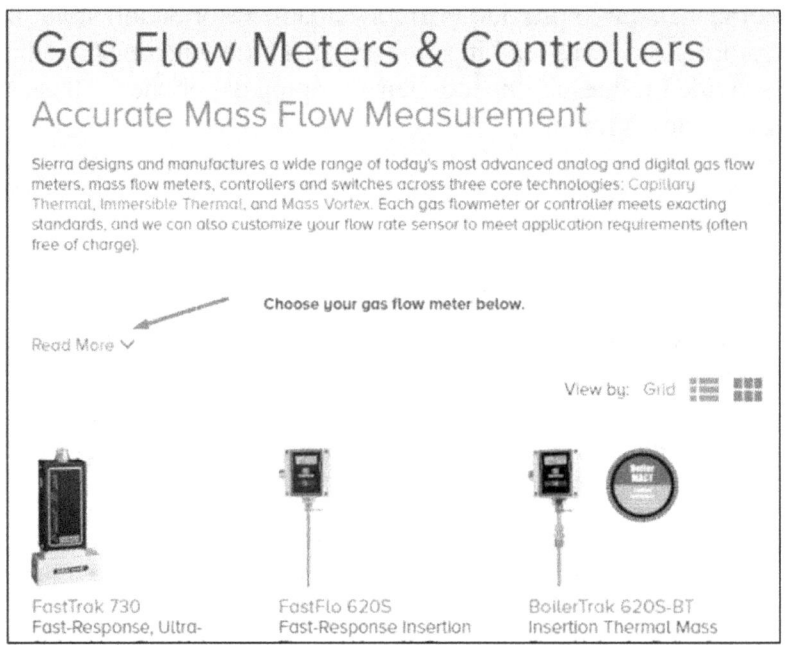

*Screen capture of SierraInstruments.com*

If you click the "Read More" link, additional text appears above the products:

*Screen capture by SierraInstruments.com*

You can make the argument as to whether or not this additional text is needed to sell the product, but assuming it is, the "read more" option is the perfect solution. The content is available to those who want it but stays out of the way for those who just want to move on to the products.

On-demand content such as this was once devalued by search engines; however, since it became common and even necessary for the mobile experience, search engines no longer treat this content any differently. At least some of the content must be visible. If all of it is hidden or otherwise invisible on the page, search engines will not consider it as part of the page.

# Displaying *n* Products Per Page

Sites with a lot of products in a single category often limit the number of products displayed on the page. To see more products, the visitor must click a "next page" link, which is typically located at the bottom of the current batch of results. This is a solution that creates even more problems.

When it comes to reducing page load speed, limiting the number of products displayed is a win. Fewer products and images per page make each page load more quickly. This is a positive result for shoppers. But what doesn't make for a good shopping experience is forcing visitors to click page after page after page to see all available products in that category. Eventually, they tire of this, and the products at the end of the list will rarely ever be seen. Not to mention, the search engines will likely visit these pages less frequently and will consider them to be less valuable. This results in a net loss.

The best option, for both visitors and search engines, is to display all your products on a single page, with on-demand image loading and strong product filtering options. Let's say you have a product category page that covers 1,000 products. If you tried to load the thumbnail images for all the products, you'd run into some serious page speed issues, frustrating shoppers. However, if you only load the images in the viewable screen area, you'll decrease the page load time significantly.

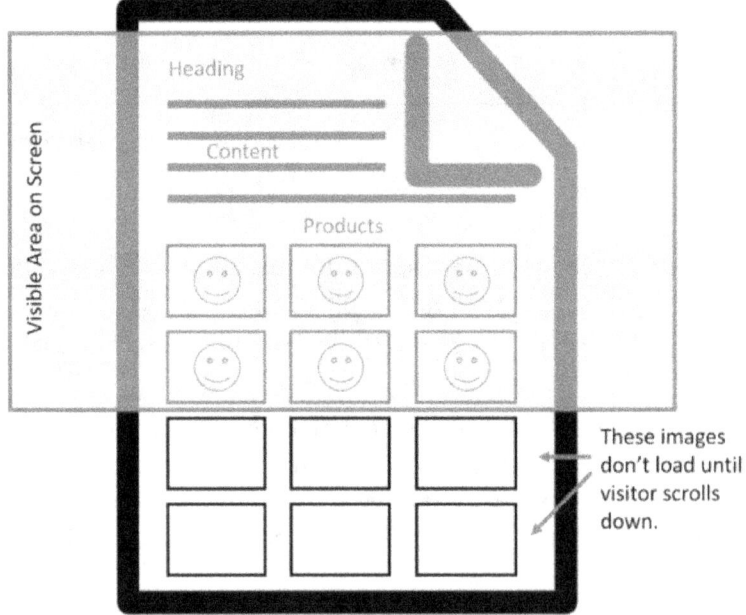

*Illustration by Stoney deGeyter*

Not only does this make more products visible without additional clicks, but it also allows the search engines to grab all your product pages without having to crawl through multiple pages. The additional load time is minimal since the images are only loading on demand.

But we still have the problem of forcing the visitor to potentially have to scroll through a thousand products to find the one they want. Some visitors are happy to do this, but most aren't. (Incidentally, visitors will still see a lot more products scrolling than they would by clicking through to the subsequent pages.)

The best way to reduce the number of products the visitor has to scroll through is to set up product filtering. Create as many filters as make sense for your products. For example, a page for ski boots might have filters for *men's*, *women's*, *boy's*, *girl's*, brand, performance, weight, height, skill level, fit, flex, buckle count, color, price, year, heated, etc. Each click of a filter will reduce the number of viewable products. This makes it easier for the shopper to find the right set of products for their need.

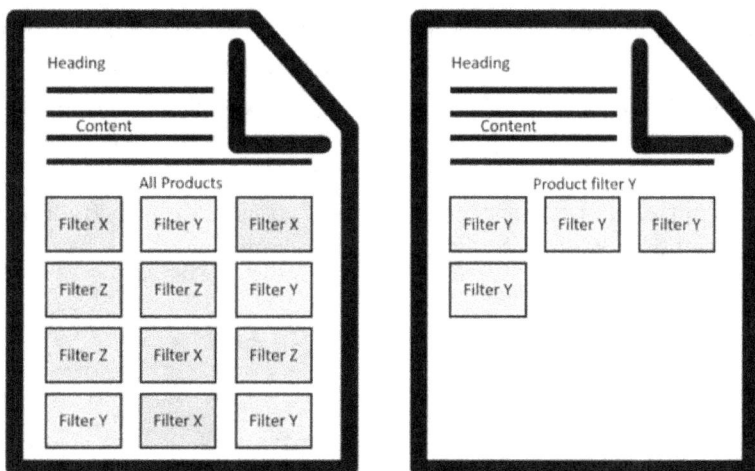

*Illustratin by Stoney deGeyter*

Use keyword research to determine which filters require their own landing pages and which can simply hide irrelevant content. For example, colors make good filters because those rarely have a lot of search volume. Visitors can filter the products in real-time without switching URLs. However, other filters, such as by brand or gender, probably deserve optimized landing pages with their own content. In the latter case, you'd send the visitor to a new more tightly focused product category page.

# Sale / Closeout Pages

One final point is important when it comes to creating a great set of optimized product category pages. Most sites focus on their product categories, forgetting that people search for those products in many different ways. A good number of searchers are often looking for your products using terms such as *discount*, *sale*, *closeout*, *deals*, etc.

We talked about optimizing for the intent of the searcher, which means that unless you only sell discount products, you don't want to drive these searchers to your main product category pages. Instead, create an *on sale* section of your site in which you then build additional landing pages for each of your product categories. The only products displayed in these categories will be those that have been reduced in price. Optimizing these landing pages is a great way to capture these discount searchers while reducing older product inventory more quickly.

## It's All About the Visitor

Product category pages are often the first line of conversion when it comes to your visitor's shopping experience. If the visitor isn't yet searching for a particular product or service, they are searching for the product category so they can learn more about the products they may want. Optimizing your product category pages not only brings more shoppers to your site, but it is also an important step to provide each shopper with a valuable on-site experience. If your product category pages don't deliver as expected, visitors leave without ever seeing the products they came for.

# PRODUCT PAGE OPTIMIZATION

In the last chapter, we focused on product category pages. Product category pages are critical to the sales process for those who don't yet know the specific product that meets their needs. For customers that do know what they are looking for, product category pages can be bypassed entirely in favor of product detail pages.

Every ecommerce product page is a potential landing page for searches that are specific to that product. If you already have the product that satisfies the searcher's intent, you should deliver the user to that product page. But product pages don't just magically appear in front of searchers to click on. Optimization is essential.

## Assign a Master Category

In the previous chapter, we placed a lot of emphasis on product categorization and optimizing those categories. Here we'll emphasize the same, but from a slightly different perspective. Product categories are designed to be the "home" for all the products that fit any particular category. But in the real world, products often have multiple homes. That is, they can fit neatly into more than one category.

As far as user experience goes, having one product in multiple categories ensures that shoppers can find the product regardless of the path they take to get there.

Let's assume for a second that a shopper is building a deck. To do so, they need lumber, concrete, a circular saw, and a book on how to do the job. We'll focus only on the book, which can be found in any one of four categories and URLs:

- Lumber > Books:
  *site.com/lumber/books/how-to-build-a-deck.html*

- Building Materials > Books:
  *site.com/building-materials/books/how-to-build-a-deck.html*

- Books > Home Projects:
  *site.com/books/home-projects/how-to-build-a-deck.html*

- Books > Decks:
  *site.com/books/decks/how-to-build-a-deck.html*

This is simplified, of course, but in this example, that one product has four "pages" competing for placement for the same search. Really, these are all just the same page found using four different paths. In SEO terms, we call this a duplicate content nightmare.

There are multiple possible solutions for this, but let's focus on the best one before getting into the less-than-stellar alternatives.

## The (Best) Solution

The best solution to this duplicate content problem is to use a CMS that allows you to assign a default master category. Using multiple categories is still an option, but only one is the canonical category. It would be this master category that determines which URL the product uses.

Using our example above, let's assign the master category Books > Decks to our book. Regardless of the path the visitor took to get to that product page, they would only land on the URL assigned to that category:

- Lumber > Books:
  *site.com/lumber/books/how-to-build-a-deck.html*

- Building Materials > Books:
  *site.com/building-materials/books/how-to-build-a-deck.html*

- Books > Home Projects:
  *site.com/books/home-projects/how-to-build-a-deck.html*

- Books > Decks:
  *site.com/books/decks/how-to-build-a-deck.html*

This eliminates the possibility of duplicate content regardless of how many categories a particular product fits into. They'll still be able to find the product through every relevant category, but the URL of the product page will never change.

Not many content management platforms support this type of solution though, which means you'll either need to look for an alternate CMS or get a programmer involved. But for large sites, this can be an important part of your long-term optimization strategy.

If this solution isn't currently a viable option for you, there are a couple of less desirable alternatives.

## Alternative Solution 1

The first alternative solution is to completely remove all category classifications from the product URLs. It looks something like this:

- *site.com/products/how-to-build-a-deck-book.html*

Rather than:

- *site.com/lumber/books/how-to-build-a-deck.html*

- *site.com/building-materials/books/how-to-build-a-deck.html*

- *site.com/books/home-projects/how-to-build-a-deck.html*

- *site.com/books/decks/how-to-build-a-deck.html*

Notice that the category name is not a part of the URL and a new category has been created for all products.

Many CMS' already support this type of framework, however, you need to be sure they don't continue to create URLs based on the shopper's path to the product.

Also, note the one significant drawback of this option is losing the category classification in the URL. That can be an important signal to the search engines to determine how the page fits into the site structure.

### Alternative Solution 2

Another alternative is to keep the CMS default settings but institute a canonical tag that points to a single "master" URL. Some CMSs by default will add canonical tags and point all relevant category URLs to the /product/ URL. While this provides a signal to the search engines telling them which URL you want to be canonical, the search engines can choose to ignore this directive. This makes this solution a gamble.

We'll go into more detail on the canonical tag a bit later.

# Fewer Landing Pages for Multi-SKU Products

Some products come in multiple shapes, sizes, colors, and other fun varieties. Each variation is essentially the same product but with slight differences that require tracking through their own SKU. For many CMSs, every SKU gets a unique URL. Even for sites with just a few products, this can result in a lot of URLs.

Below is an example of a site that has one product, a "T-Rex Hates" shirt design, with 52 different styles, 19 colors and 5 sizes. If you do the math on that, you're looking at 4940 unique URLs to cover each variation of this single product.

Here is a sampling:

- *site.com/trex-hates_tshirt?productId=1321218904#color=navy/white&size=medium*

- *site.com/trex-hates_tshirt?productId=1321218904#color=green&size=x-large*

- *site.com/trex-hates_tshirt?productId=1321218904#color=red&size=3x-large tall*

Of the almost 5000 URLs, how many can we eliminate without a negative impact to customers finding the product they want through search? Probably all but four, and possibly all but one.

## The (Best) Solution

"T-Rex Hates" comes in four unique styles: T-Shirt, Jersey, Long-Sleeve, and Golf Shirt. But if we perform a bit of keyword research, we find that most people are only searching for "*t rex hates shirt*" or "*t rex hates t shirt,*" which tells us we really could drop this to one primary style with the others as selectable options.

And what about the color and size options? These can be keywords used in search, but they are far less common. There is no reason to require a unique URL for those options to get the product to show up in those searches.

This means we have boiled almost 5000 URLs down to a single URL without removing any style, size, or color options. When a shopper selects the options they want, the URL doesn't need to change, even if a separate SKU is required. The database can track all the variables selected and send the appropriate SKU.

Here is a site that has similar products and is set up correctly, at least in terms of the sizing options. Notice the two images below show the change in SKU based on the selection of the shirt size. Changing the options doesn't change the URL, just the SKU displayed.

Sad T-Rex | Clap Your Oh
Men's T-Shirt

$22.00

SKU:
GT2339-101BLK-S

* Size:
S    M    L    XL    2XL    3XL
4XL

Sad T-Rex | Clap Your Oh
Men's T-Shirt

$23.00

SKU:
GT2339-101BLK-2XL

* Size:
S    M    L    XL    2XL    3XL
4XL

*Screen captures by Stoney deGeyter*

Again, not all systems work this way and yours may require extensive reprogramming or a new ecommerce solution altogether that will give you the optimization flexibility you need. But of all possible fixes, this is the best and most error-proof option. That said, there are (less desirable) alternatives.

## Alternative Solution 1

We talked a bit about the canonical tag above. This is another place it can be used. Simply add a canonical tag on every URL variation and point it to the "primary" product URL. The site example we used above for the TRex Hates Shirt has thousands of URLs for the same product, but they point all of those product variations to one URL: *site.com/trex-hates_tshirt*. Each style has a self-referential canonical tag, which is a perfectly acceptable way to do this if they want each style to be a unique landing page.

But once again, the downside of this approach is that the canonical tag is only a hint. Not only can search engines choose to ignore it, but they can also use a great deal of your daily crawl budget spidering thousands of URLs that won't achieve rankings.

### Alternative Solution 2

The next less-preferred option is to use Google Search Console (and Bing Webmaster Central) to tell the engines to ignore the specific parameters tagged onto the end of the URLs. Parameters are everything to the left of a *?* in a URL.

In this URL (*site.com/trex-hates_tshirt?productId=1321218904#color=navy/white&size=medium*), you can see the following parameters:

- Product ID
- Color
- Size

You can tell Google to ignore each or all of these. This lets Google know that the canonical URL is *site.com/trex-hates_tshirt* and they can ignore the rest. The obvious downside here is that what you tell Google only applies to Google, and this process has to be duplicated with each search engine.

You also need to be extremely careful not to ignore needed parameters. For example, if the site uses a particular parameter to differentiate between styles, and you want to keep those as separate landing pages, then you should not exclude that parameter from Google.

You'll want to check each parameter to know how it's used and see how vital it is to display products properly. A single misstep in parameter exclusion can have devastating consequences.

# Canonical Tag

We've already mentioned the canonical tag as an alternate solution for a couple of issues, but we'll address it in more detail here.

The canonical tag is a simple line of code that tells the search engines which URL is the "true" URL when there are multiple duplicate pages available. Here's what a full canonical tag looks like:

*<link rel="canonical" href="http://www.site.com/everything-else-goes-here">*

Search engines use this tag as a signal, but not as an absolute directive. They can choose to ignore it if they want. They will ignore your canonical tag if they believe that the content on another URL is substantially different from the URL the canonical points to. You can tell the search engines your preference, but you can't force them to adhere to it. Even when using a canonical tag, your site is still vulnerable to many of the issues inherent with duplicate content.

So while it's good practice to use canonical tags across your site, it's nothing more than a band-aid solution for the previously mentioned issues. Think of it as a backup plan in the case that something goes awry.

# Titles and Descriptions

Unless you have come up with your own line of products, you're very likely to sell similar items that are also sold on hundreds or thousands of other stores. If you do have your own product line, there's a good chance they are being sold on multiple websites across the web. In either of these scenarios, you're either getting your product descriptions from the manufacturer or you're writing product descriptions for the other sellers. Which means you're likely publishing duplicate titles and descriptions on your site.

When search engines see hundreds of products with essentially the same information, they have to decide which one of those pages should rank over the other. Typically, the site with the greatest authority wins. If that's not you, you'll be buried behind many other sites in the search results.

Even if you don't rewrite the product descriptions, you can make your site stand out with custom product titles and descriptions. Yes, this is time-consuming when you have thousands of products, but without making this basic effort, there's just no way to stand out in search. In many cases it is possible to write titles and descriptions that appear to be unique by using values from the database to fill in templates. Consider doing just this if you don't have time to write custom titles and descriptions for all of your products.

Creating unique content allows you to create a distinguishing voice that sets you apart from the other sellers. Use that voice throughout your site. Be fun, be creative, be authoritative—whatever works for you. But by all means, add value!

## Alternate Solution

If writing unique titles and meta descriptions for all of your products is out of reach, the next option is to find a way to get unique content onto your product pages. Content that no one else has. Try soliciting user-generated content from your customers. This can be in the form of product reviews, case studies, videos of the product in use, etc. Anything you can do to differentiate your content from your competitors will earn you the opportunity to stand out from the crowd.

And while we are on that topic...

# User-Generated Content

Publishing user-generated content (UGC) on your product pages isn't just a failsafe for when you can't make your own content unique. Even if you've written unique titles, descriptions, and product information for all your products, UGC is one more tool in your arsenal to increase the value of your product pages.

Search engines tend to visit frequently updated pages more often. They are not interested in cosmetic changes; only changes that warrant re-indexing. UGC is a solid way to get them coming back. If the UGC is topically focused (and it should be) this can help push your pages further up in the search results.

UGC comes in a variety of formats. You can decide which are right for your site, but I would consider each of them and implement all you can:

**Reviews** - Allow shoppers to write reviews of your products/services.

**Ratings** - Similar to reviews, you can also have shoppers rate your products.

**Questions** - Some shoppers have questions they need answers to before they feel comfortable making the purchase. Providing a space to ask those questions not only increases the likelihood of getting that sale, but it also helps other shoppers who have the same question.

**Stories** - Let visitors post their own experiences with your product or service. This is less of a review than it is a way to highlight creative ways your products were used and what solutions they solved.

**Pictures** - Along with stories, you can let your visitors post pictures that show your products in use.

**Videos** - Video has never been more popular, and people love creating them. Let customers upload a video to tell their stories and show your product being used. If a picture is worth a thousand words, a video is worth even more.

# Schema / Structured Data Markup

Structured data (or schema) markup allows you to tag certain types of content with coded labels that tell the search engines how to "interpret" it. Search engines are pretty good at reading long-form content, but the data placed in smaller snippets can often get lost in formatting. Schema helps the search engines read the content in context and better understand its meaning. And in many cases, they'll promote that content in their search results visually.

Let's say that you display SKU numbers on your product pages. The visitor may be able to scan the page and pull out the SKU number, but the search engine may not be able to tell the SKU number from all the other data on the page. Schema fixes that and ensures there is no room for ambiguity on how that content is read.

New schema is being created every day, so you'll want to review schema.org for relevant schema options you can implement. Here are a few specific to product pages:

- Product name
- Product image
- Product description
- Brand
- Reviews
- Ratings
- Special offers
- SKUs
- Price
- Currency
- Availability
- URL

# User-Focused Optimization

Thus far, the strategies addressed in this chapter have been related to search engines. Just about everything outlined above can be a boon for helping your site visitors in one way or another, but now we want to focus specifically on user experience optimization.

Without visitors, our websites are nothing. It doesn't matter how beautiful, how great the content, or how "optimized" it is, if the visitors are not having a good experience, it's all for naught. So, let's give visitors more of what they want so they have a great on-site experience.

## Consistent Layout

The layout of your product pages should be relatively consistent across the board. Occasionally you may have a group of products that requires unique information blocks, but as much as possible, keep your product templates as similar as possible. This allows shoppers to easily scan through multiple products and identify key pieces of information without having to re-learn where each piece is located.

## Multiple Image Views

Many product pages can be enhanced by providing multiple product image views. Will shoppers benefit from seeing the product from a different angle, enlarged, or in use? If so, add additional images they can peruse.

This may not be necessary for every type of product, but for most, an additional image or two gives the customer a better idea if it's right for them. The more comfortable the customer is with the purchase, the less likely they are to return it.

## Product Availability

Nobody wants to add a product to their cart only to find out later that it's currently unavailable. Provide an "in stock" or "out of stock" indicator as shown below to let shoppers know whether or not they will be able to complete their purchase. If the available quantity is limited, displaying the number of items remaining can be a great motivator to purchase the product now, rather than waiting.

*Screen capture by Stoney deGeyter*

## Add to Cart Proximity

Place your "Add to Cart" buttons near the product price. When the cart button is in an unexpected location, shoppers tend to miss or gloss over it. Check the button placement in varying screen sizes and resolutions, as these factors can move information to places you didn't intend.

Depending on your products, you may want to allow customers to add products to a wishlist or save them for later viewing. If the shopper isn't ready to buy, this can be a nice reminder the next time they log in.

Similarly, an option to forward the page via email, text or social can get the customer back to your store when the time is right or provide an easy way to share the product with a friend.

## Security Assurances

Every shopper that visits your site for the first time has a trust hurdle to overcome. If your website does not establish trust, you diminish your opportunity to secure sales. You must actively address and alleviate customers' trust concerns in as many ways as possible.

*Screen capture by Stoney deGeyter*

Here are a handful of trust concerns that your product pages need to answer:

- Do you take credit cards?
- Do you take my preferred form of payment?
- Will my personal information be protected?
- How long will the product take to arrive?
- What is your return policy?

- Do you offer guarantees?
- If I have a problem, will I talk to a real person?
- Will my personal information be secure?
- Will my information be used to spam me?

Eliminates opportunities for the customer to walk away before purchasing by addressing each of these issues. Provide the answers before the customer knows they have any concerns to to secure their business.

## Cross Promotion

Product cross-promotion can increase the average order value of each order placed. Whether you offer impulse buys or expose customers to related products they may not have known about, showing these additional products increases the odds of customers throwing an additional item into their cart. Cross-promotions may be the only exposure customers get to these highly relevant products they may want or need.

*Screen capture by Stoney deGeyter*

## Keep the Shopper Shopping

Imagine for a second that you're in a grocery store. But the store doesn't allow you to keep your cart with you as you browse the aisles. Instead, you have to leave the cart at the end of each aisle as you browse the shelves. Each time you grab an item you have to walk back to your cart. And you can only add one unique product at a time.

Any store that demanded that would likely not get you to return, no matter how many deals they offer. But this is exactly what web sites do when they force visitors to visit the cart page every time they add an item. Switching pages forces them out of the aisle where they are shopping, requiring them to "walk back" to the page they were on to continue their shopping experience.

When customers add products to the cart, provide a notification it's been added, but let the visitor continue shopping from where they are. When they are ready to look at the cart, they will. Otherwise, keep them shopping.

## Facilitate Socialization

In the age of social media, people like to broadcast what's going on in their life. This includes what they're buying. Shoppers are far more likely to share a product on their favorite social platform than they are to write a review. These social posts can act as mini-reviews and they are free marketing that you would not have gotten otherwise. But this can only happen if you make it easy to socialize your products.

Be sure your products have socialization options (like the one shown below) for your audience's favorite social platforms. It's a simple step that turns your customers into product evangelists.

*Screen capture by Stoney deGeyter*

You can take socialization one step further by offering a Twitter or RSS feed that regularly pushes out new product information, offers, and sales. You may be surprised when these feeds become more popular than your regular social channels!

# Ecommerce Tracking

Finally, no optimization would be complete without making sure your ecommerce tracking is installed and tracking properly. It is important to understand how visitors interact on your product pages, what they buy, and where they exit. You can use this data to improve the shoppers' on-site experience. Spend time analyzing and removing any hurdle that you find common among your shoppers.

Often the most valuable time spent on marketing and promotion is optimizing product pages. One of the best things about optimizing product pages is that almost all of the changes you need to make are template related. You can optimize hundreds or even thousands of pages with a few small template tweaks. Product pages are usually the last stop before a visitor makes a purchase or leaves the site. Optimizing these pages can make or break your conversion rates. This often makes product page optimization the best bang for your buck in terms of your marketing efforts. A few improvements here can make all the difference for your business.

# STRUCTURED DATA OPTIMIZATION

Structured data, also known as schema markup, was introduced in 2011 through Schema.org, a joint effort between Google, Yahoo, and Bing. It was built to help search engines better understand certain types of content.

The importance of structured data is growing day-by-day as new schema is developed . Implemented properly, schema provides an opportunity for webmasters to get key pieces of information to appear in search results.

Implementing structured data on your pages doesn't guarantee search engines will display the content you've marked up, but it does increase the chances it will appear. There are a myriad of ever-changing ways search engines may choose to display this data.

The image below shows several rich snippets appearing in a single search result.

*Screen capture from Google.com*

Using schema markup doesn't give you direct control over what search engines choose to display, but at the very least, it opens the door to more enhanced listings. Not only does it  enable your site to stand out, but it can also provide valuable information to the searcher that may influence their purchase decision.

As a shopper, which of the two results below holds greater appeal?

Young Living Diffuser Accessories and Tools | Young Living Essential ...
https://www.youngliving.com/en_US/products/diffusers-accessories/tools ▾
Discover the transformative, aromatic power of essential oils throughout your home. Our diffusers let you reap the benefits of essential oil aromatherapy in any ...
Rainstone Diffuser · Aria Ultrasonic Diffuser · Bamboo Diffuser · USB Orb™ Diffuser

Amazon.com: Essential Oil Diffuser Riverock, Aromatherapy Oil Spa ...
https://www.amazon.com/Essential-Aromatherapy-Humidifier.../dp/B00L9NR672 ▾
★★★★☆ Rating: 4.6 - 2,878 reviews
Buy Essential Oil Diffuser Riverock, Aromatherapy Oil Spa Humidifier and Ultrasonic Mister. Perfect Decor Gift for a Peaceful Home Yoga Meditation Workout or ...

*Screen capture from Google.com*

The second, right? That's the power of schema markup. It can improve your click-through rates, and if your site has schema when others above you don't, it can even generate a higher number of clicks than sites that rank higher.

# Schema Formats

There are three types of schema:

- Microdata
- JSON-LD
- RDFa

The first two are the most popular and will probably suffice for most of your needs. While the implementation of each type of schema looks different, they accomplish the same goal. Below are two examples. If you're not a code junkie, the images below won't have a lot of meaning to you, but they do demonstrate the implementation difference.

Microdata is typically added around the items you're describing, and JSON-LD is included in a separate script tag. If this is all Greek to you, just let your developer know what you are trying to accomplish and they will take care of it.

## Microdata:

```
<div itemscope itemtype="http://schema.org/Product">
  <span itemprop="brand">ACME</span> <span itemprop="name">Executive Anvil</span>
  <img itemprop="image" src="anvil_executive.jpg" />

  <span itemprop="aggregateRating" itemscope itemtype="http://schema.org/AggregateRating">
    Average rating: <span itemprop="ratingValue">4.4</span>, based on
    <span itemprop="ratingCount">89</span> reviews
  </span>

  <span itemprop="offers" itemscope itemtype="http://schema.org/AggregateOffer">
    from $<span itemprop="lowPrice">119.99</span> to
    $<span itemprop="highPrice">199.99</span>
    <meta itemprop="priceCurrency" content="USD" />
  </span>
</div>
```

*Screen capture by Stoney deGeyter*

# JSON-LD:

```
<script type='application/ld+json'>
{
  "@context": "http://www.schema.org",
  "@type": "ChildCare",
  "name": "I Don't (Child) Care",
  "url": "www.notarealsite.com",
  "logo": "logoimage.com",
  "image": "businessimage.com",
  "description": "We don't do child care because we really don't care.",
  "address": {
    "@type": "PostalAddress",
    "streetAddress": "1234 Nowhere St.",
    "addressLocality": "Nothingville",
    "addressRegion": "CA",
    "postalCode": "44444",
    "addressCountry": "USA"
  },
  "openingHours": "Mo 23:30-23:59 Tu -",
  "contactPoint": {
    "@type": "ContactPoint",
    "contactType": "me",
    "telephone": "333-333-3333"
  }
}
</script>
```

*Screen capture by Stoney deGeyter*

# RDFa:

```
<div typeof="foaf:Person" xmlns:foaf="http://xmlns.com/
foaf/0.1/">
    <p property="foaf:name">
     Alice Birpemswick
    </p>
    <p>
     Email: <a rel="foaf:mbox"
href="mailto:alice@example.com">alice@example.com</a>
    </p>
    <p>
     Phone: <a rel="foaf:phone" href="tel:
+1-617-555-7332">+1 617.555.7332</a>
    </p>
</div>
```

*Screen capture by Stoney deGeyter*

# Implementing Schema

Structured data isn't difficult to implement, and several tools make it easy, but you'll want to verify accurate implementation using a validator of some kind. If you don't want to rely on third-party tools then get your developer involved and add the markup directly to your code.

According to schema.org, here are the most commonly used schema:

- Creative works: Creative Work, Book, Movie, Music Recording, Recipe, TV Series, etc.
- Embedded non-text objects: Audio Object, Image Object, Video Object
- Event
- Health and medical types: notes on the health and medical types under Medical Entity.
- Organization
- Person
- Place, Local Business, Restaurant ...
- Product, Offer, Aggregate Offer
- Review, Aggregate Rating
- Action

It's important to choose the right markup tags for your specific vertical or industry. Here are some common page types and the schema most often used:

**Ecommerce Sites**

- Product Rating
- Product Reviews
- Price
- Availability
- Similar Products

**Local Business Sites**

- NAP (name, address, phone number)
- Reviews
- Hours of operation

- Price range (not relevant for some businesses)

**Events**

- Rating/Review of ticket broker (not applicable for all events)
- Date
- Performer
- Location

**Booking Travel**

- Availability
- Price
- Rating

Once you've implemented and validated your schema, keep an eye on the results. You'll be happy to see it show up in the search results. If something goes wrong, you'll need to correct it right away.

And remember, new schema is regularly added, so be sure to keep an eye on changes in your industry and take advantage of any new opportunities as they arise.

# PDF OPTIMIZATION

When it comes to optimizing your site's content for search engine rankings, nothing beats a web page. But not every type of content is best suited for web viewing. Long-form and formatted content often works better as a downloadable PDF. PDFs should never be used when a web page will do, but there are some definite benefits to using PDFs in the right situations.

## When to Use PDFs on the Web

In most instances, a web page provides you all the flexibility you need to deliver your content in a visually appealing layout. But a web page doesn't work for every situation, especially if you need or want visitors to download, print, or share precisely formatted content. Here are some typical types of content that you may want to publish as a PDF instead of a web page.

**Articles over 3000 words -** There's nothing wrong with a long-form blog post, but at some point, your content may be better formatted as a downloadable e-book with illustrations and graphics. PDFs give you precise control for how your content looks. They also allow you to add cover art, along with headers and footers, just like a normal book. PDFs can also be passed on via email attachments rather than as links to web pages.

**Specification Documents -** Specification docs are often very format heavy, relying on images, illustrations, tables, and graphs. These can make the PDF format valuable. However, unless your customers frequently print this material, a web page will often suffice, making the PDF unnecessary.

**White Papers -** Similar to e-books, white papers are usually long-form content that is better provided as a download to print, but you may want to also make this available to read on a screen.

**Any Offline Content -** Any content that is better read offline rather than online can be made into a PDF. In fact, any info-heavy blog post can benefit by being turned into a downloadable PDF in addition to being available online, for those who want to read it away from their screens. However, if you take this route, be aware of the potential for duplicate content.

If you decide that PDFs are preferred, or even necessary, over a typical web page (and they are not locked behind form submissions or paywalls), you'll want to optimize them for visitors and possibly even search engines.

# Optimize for Search and Clicks

Quite often, PDFs are used as downloadable content offered in exchange for an email address or subscription opt-in. Since PDFs such as these are generally behind a subscription or paywall, there is no need for them to be optimized for search. If that's the only type of PDF content you produce, feel free to skip this section and move on to the next.

Still here?

Great, that means you want to make your PDFs indexable and ready to rank for search.

Optimizing PDFs is very different than a web page. You'll need a copy of Adobe Acrobat Pro to do all of these optimizations, but most of it can be done with the free version.

## Use Text-Based Files

Search engines don't read text in images well. Just like a web page, your optimized PDFs must use standard text that the search engines can read. Images and illustrations are great for adding visual flair, but the bulk of the content needs to be text.

## Search-Friendly File Names

The PDF file name is akin to the URL of a web page. Save the PDF using relevant keywords separated by hyphens rather than spaces. In most cases, the PDF file name will be part of the URL used to access the document.

If your original Word document is: *Complete Guide for PDF Optimization.docx*

Your PDF file name should read: *complete-guide-pdf-optimization.pdf*

## Optimize Your Content

Optimize your PDF content for the keyword topics you want to rank for just like any other optimized web page. Follow all the standard content optimization procedures regarding keyword usage, heading tags, etc.

## Add Alt Text to Images

With Acrobat Pro, you can add alt text to your PDF images similarly to a web page. The process is different, but the value is the same.

Using this tool, you can find all the images in the document without any alt text and add it to each image. Be succinct but descriptive, using keywords when warranted.

## Optimize PDF Properties

While web pages have meta information, PDFs have optimizable titles, descriptions, and other properties as shown below:

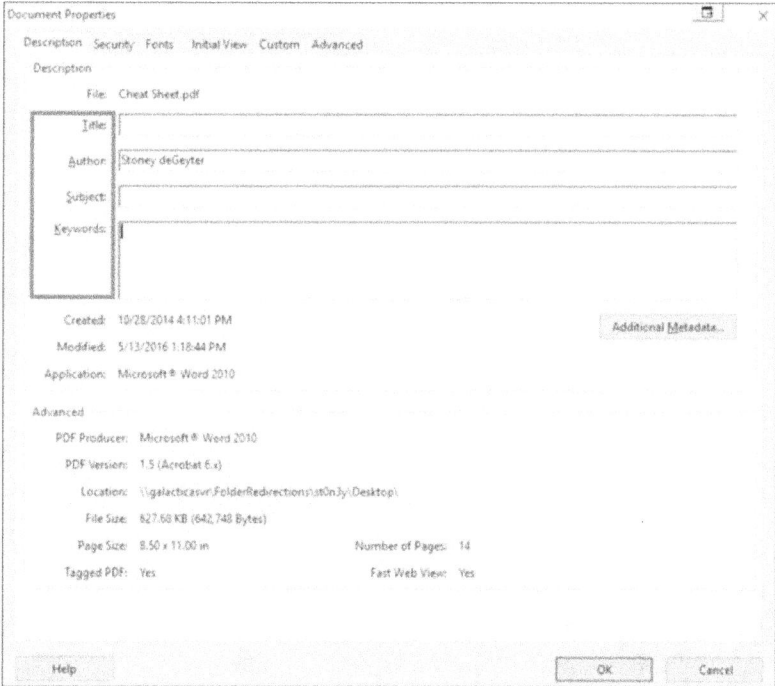

*Screen capture of Adobe Reader*

The title property is equivalent to the title tag of a web page. This will be what the search engines show as the clickable link when the PDF appears in the search results. As with any title, you should optimize this for keywords and entice visitors to click it.

The remaining fields have little to no search impact and can be ignored. However, you may want to treat the subject similar to a meta description. You never know if the search engines will choose to use that to support your optimized title when displaying your PDF in search results.

There is also an "Additional Metadata" button that will pull from the title and description you just created, but it also gives you some additional options. One thing you may wish to utilize is copyright status. Change that to Copyrighted or Public Domain, based on what fits the document, and add a copyright notice in the box. It's unlikely any of this has an impact on search, but it can't hurt to fill these in to protect your publication.

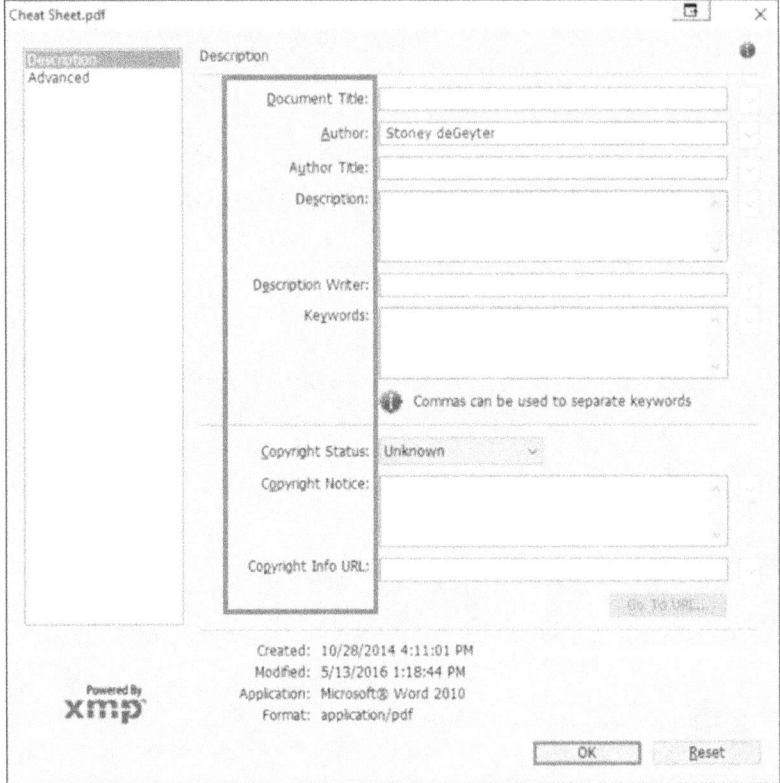

*Screen capture of Adobe Reader*

And finally, on the Advanced tab is a place to set the PDFs language. This is important if creating PDF documents in multiple languages.

## Link Out of Your PDF

Since you're optimizing the PDF for web viewing, you may as well add some strategic links to your website. Be sure to use relevant anchor text so when your PDF is indexed, the links will carry value in search like standard web page links do.

If your PDF is primarily for off-line viewing (print), you will want to use the link URL rather than (or in addition to) the linked keyword text. This will at least give printed-page readers a way to visit the reference if they are inclined to type the full URL into their browser later.

## Check Compatibility

When you save your PDF, be sure it's compatible with older versions of Acrobat. I suggest you go a couple of versions lower than the latest to ensure most readers or search engines will be able to view the document.

## Link to Your PDF

Search engines find documents and pages via links from other web pages. If you hope to have your PDF found and indexed, you'll need to link to it from your website's content.

# PDF File Size Compression

You should have your visitors in mind with any optimization that you do. Aside from the optimizing the content, you should ensure that you reduce the file size of the PDF . Larger documents will always take longer to download, but if you reduce that time as much as possible, you will do your audience a favor.

The first step is to look in the PDF settings to see if it's been optimized yet:

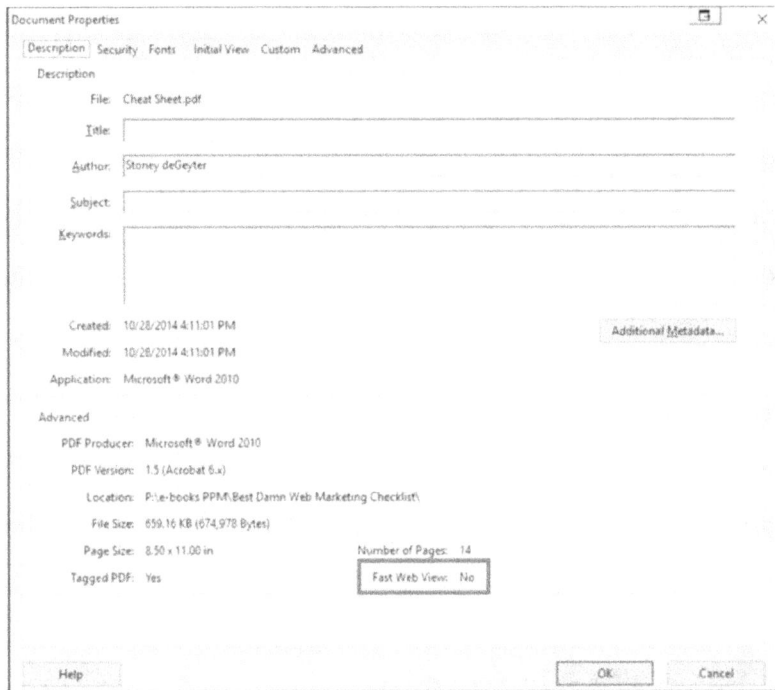

*Screen capture of Adobe Reader*

If it hasn't, you know what you need to do. Read below to learn how you do it.

## Optimize Fonts

**Use Standard Fonts -** All PDF readers support a set of standard fonts: Times, Helvetica, Courier, Symbol, and Zapf Dingbats. Any other fonts you use will likely have to be embedded, which increases the PDF file size.

**Use Fewer Fonts -** Every font you use in your document adds kilobytes to your file. Keep your font variables down to as few as possible.

**Limit Font Styles -** Not only does using more fonts increase the size, but also every font style is treated the same as a unique font. So if you have even just one usage of italics, bold, or bold italics, you're adding kilobytes. This becomes especially important when using non-standard fonts that have to be embedded. Each style variation is a new font embed.

## Optimize Images

**Use Vector-Based Images -** Whenever possible, use vector-based image files. These are smaller and higher quality than bitmaps.

**Use Monochrome Bitmap Images -** If you can't use vector-based images, make your bitmaps monochrome rather than full-color. This will keep the images as small as possible.

## Reduce PDF Size

**Save as Minimum Size -** When saving a Word document to PDF format, ensure the PDF is created in the smallest size possible. Look at your save options to verify that "ISO 19005-1 compliant (PDF/A)" and "Bitmap text when fonts may not be embedded" are not checked, as shown below.

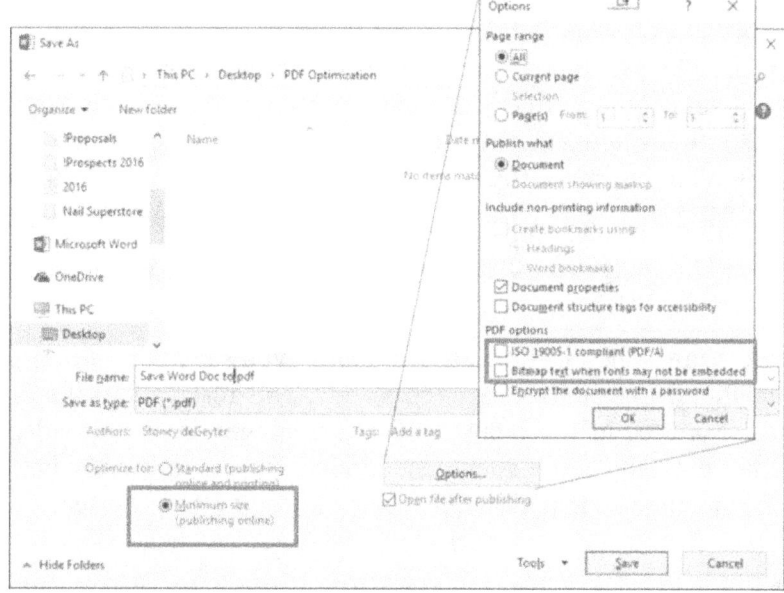

*Screen capture of Adobe Reader*

## Optimize in Adobe Acrobat

If you have Adobe Acrobat Pro, you can further optimize your newly created PDF. You have several options to reduce the file size of your PDF document. The PDF will likely already be set to "Standard" mode. Then select "Mobile" mode, or create your own custom presets.

*Screen capture of Adobe Reader*

Adobe provides a helpful tutorial on how to utilize the different panels, so let's not recreate the wheel here. Adjust the custom settings to your liking to maximize speed optimization without sacrificing quality, and you're all set. Then it's just a matter of saving and naming your custom settings if you want to retain those for future use.

If you have a lot of PDFs to optimize, you may want to have custom settings based on the content of the PDF. Image-rich PDFs will probably need different optimization settings than text-heavy PDFs.

> **Fast Web View:** There is one last step before you save your newly optimized PDF, and that is to enable "Fast Web View." This restructures the PDF so that when it's requested in a web environment, the pages are downloaded one at a time, rather than the entire document at once. This is especially important for large PDF documents that are likely to be viewed in the browser.

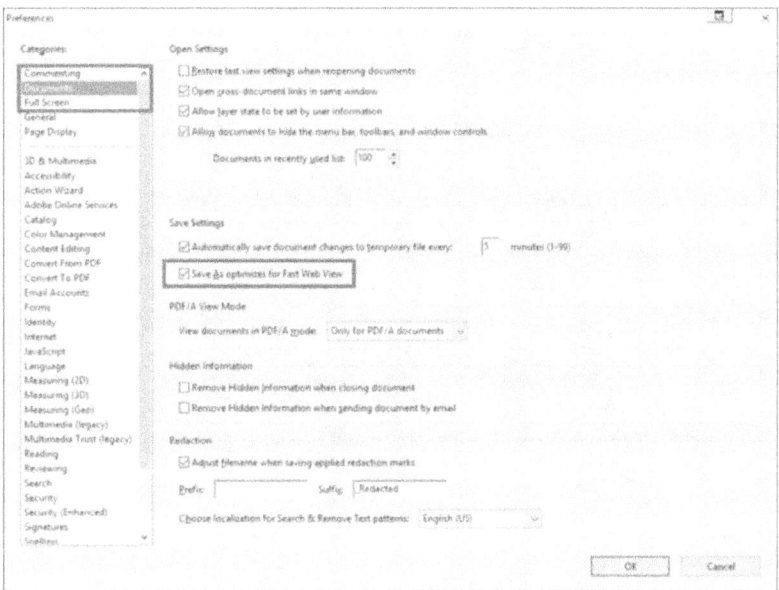

*Screen capture of Adobe Reader*

Now when you save, you can go back to view the properties and see a "Yes" next to "Fast Web View."

Still not convinced you have the smallest PDF file possible? There are many tools available such as Smallpdf and PDFCompressor that you can use to try to compress your PDF even further, though your results may vary.

**Initial View Settings:** Adobe also gives you options to set how you want the PDF to be seen upon being opened. Here you can set whether or not the navigation tab is open by default, the visible page layout, window size, and other options.

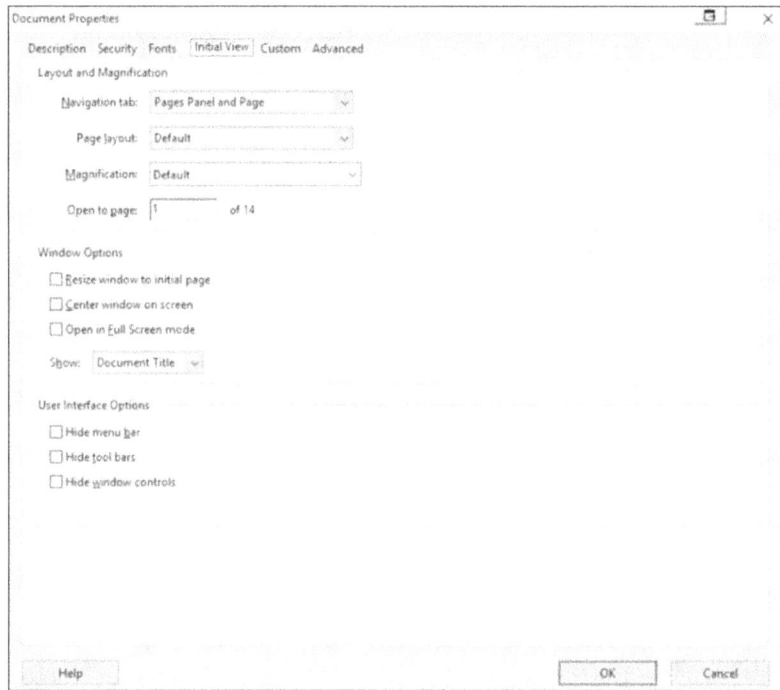

*Screen capture of Adobe Reader*

# Don't Overlook PDF Optimization

While marketers often create PDFs for various web marketing campaigns, PDF optimization is easy to overlook. Unfortunately, this is to the overall detriment of the optimization campaign's success.

Take a few extra minutes to follow the steps above and ensure your PDFs will be both people and search-engine friendly. This gives you the greatest opportunity for exposure and download.

# CONCLUDING REMARKS

The process of website optimization is broad, and I couldn't possibly contain it all in one book.. What I have outlined in the previous chapters covers only a small portion of the research and strategies you need to employ to improve your web presence. But it does cover the most common and important tactics.

In my previous digital marketing book, *The Best Damn Web Marketing Checklist, Period!*, I focused on the "what to do" in digital marketing. That book was designed to act as a checklist (gasp!) of all the things that you need to remember to execute an effective digital marketing strategy. In this book, I focused on the "how to do it" aspects of digital marketing. I tried to avoid getting too deep into the technical nature of things since that can, and often does, change with search engine algorithm updates. But even still, you may find some things slightly different today than when this was written.

Changes such as pixel counts in title tags or meta description word limits do not invalidate the strategies presented here. Almost everything mentioned in this book has been true for years and will continue to be true for years to come. These are foundational aspects of digital marketing that you must remember and adhere to, although you can tweak them slightly with time.

Now that you have read this book, you hopefully feel comfortable enough to apply these improvements to your website. If not, you are still ahead of the game simply because now you know what needs to be done. If you can't do certain things yourself, don't hesitate to reach out to your developer or digital marketing agency for help with the actual implementation.

Now go forth and master your website optimization!

# ABOUT THE AUTHOR

Stoney deGeyter has been a digital marketer before there was even a term for it. In fact, he started optimizing websites for search engines before there was Google. With over 21 years of hands-on, practical experience, Stoney has helped hundreds of businesses build a successful online presence in competitive digital landscapes. He leads teams, develops strategies, organizes processes, analyzes goals, and produces results that drive leads, sales, revenues, and profits.

With expertise in website architecture, content optimization, user experience, social media, content marketing strategy, paid advertising, and analytics, Stoney pushes digital marketing teams to the next level.

Stoney is dedicated to the improvement of the digital marketing community. He's written thousands of articles for Search Engine Journal, Marketing Land, Search Engine Land, and his own company blog. Stoney speaks regularly at marketing and other national conferences to help brands grow their online authority through strategic and effective digital marketing strategies.

He's also the author of *The Best Damn Web Marketing Checklist, Period!*, the go-to desk reference for digital marketing processes that keeps managers and strategists on task, leaving no stone unturned and no essential overlooked on their way to success.